EXPLANATION IN SOCIAL SCIENCE

A System Paradigm

THE DORSEY SERIES IN POLITICAL SCIENCE

EDITOR NORTON E. LONG *Brandeis University*

EXPLANATION IN SOCIAL SCIENCE

A System Paradigm

EUGENE J. MEEHAN

Brandeis University

1968 • THE DORSEY PRESS • Homewood, Illinois

First Printing, January, 1968
Second Printing, September, 1968

Library of Congress Catalog Card No. 68–17375

Printed in the United States of America

In a most important way, the foundation of a subject is its epistemology. Social science insofar as it has warrant comprises a variety of ways of knowing about a range of phenomena. Quite literally the science amounts to how we think we know in the area to which it relates. The paradigm of knowledge invoked is central to the provision of standards, and these standards guide and govern inquiry. The analytic, deductive ideal of subsuming particular cases under universal laws has been a millstone around the neck of social science. It has occasioned the search for statistical generalizations which, despite acceptance of Hume's argument, could be used to substitute for timeless laws and illegitimately found a base for logical inference. More—since social science can boast of few, if any, timeless laws—it has set an ideal which is frustratingly unrealizable and misdirects inquiry. Natural science, having antedated the currently fashionable philosophy of science, has maintained successful procedures despite their implicit and explicit contradiction of philosophic precepts. Social science, envious, and rightly, of natural science attainments, has sought to imitate its elder. Unfortunately, the model taken for imitation has been the artifact of the philosophers of science rather than the actual practice of scientists. The present essay seeks to remedy this by providing a paradigm of knowledge which is far more in accord with the actual practice of natural science; but this aside, and far more important, it provides a useful model of knowledge for the social sciences.

What the writer has done is to fasten on explanation as the basis of the knowing enterprise. Explanation entails a patterning of variables and their logical relationships, such that given the stated interactional rules, the phenomenon to be explained would logically result when the variables were given assigned values. The phenomenon in the explanation is logically entailed. This is the sense in which we predict, and the only sense in which we can do so with logical warrant. It is in no sense different from the schoolboy's algebra for calculating the progress of a boat on a stream. The logic applies to the relations in the formula. Its usefulness for understanding and controlling events in the real world depends on the isomorphism of the variables and their relations to the relevant natural phenomena. The question is whether it fits the case. If it applies, the loaded calculus has predictive power for the natural state situation. It thus permits, at least in principle, intervention or, in the sense of Karl Popper, falsification.

Now what this view has to say for social science is that the knowing process is one not of passively awaiting, or even actively seeking, an n of statistical instances to alert the observer to a uniformity of nature, but of seizing on the intuition of a patterning in any phenomena and turning this insight into testable and tested theory. The theory, the explanation, provides a logically related set of variables entailing the phenomena. Its interest lies in its power to predict outcomes when properly loaded. Its logical coercion is purely internal to the specified relationships. Its applicability is bounded by the range of phenomena for which it has explanatory power. Social science seen this way is a set of patterned variables whose logical relationships entail the phenomena whose explanation interests the social scientist.

Men have always sought to understand human behavior
by going to history. Historical analogies are the stock-in-
trade of statesmen and of academicians as well. History
both has lessons and is said to have no lesson. Both of
these positions may be right in the sense that history
has many lessons but no lesson. From the point of view
of a nonmetaphysical social science, the lessons of history
are what is important. The lessons of history that might be
important are the explanations of significant events that
lie buried and unexplicated in the implicit organization
of the historian's tale. The reader's insight of a pattern
that might give a logic to a train of events, not only explaining the events in question but perhaps applying
elsewhere, is the tantalizing appeal of history for the
social scientist. In the past, few historians have cared to
expose to view the logic by virtue of which they found
their arrangement of events persuasive. Some contemporary historians have begun to recognize that the explanatory power, and thus the value, of their histories depends
on the model of events that they use explicitly or implicitly to order the phenomena to which they attend;
and they realize that rendering it explicit is vastly helpful
in its testing and improvement.

Political scientists have been scarcely more willing than
historians to make explicit the logical mechanisms on
which they depend for such explanations as they possess.
This is partly due to a paternity that still sees much of
political science engaged in contemporary institutional
historiography. A novelistic richness of detail, combined
with the plausibility of an uncoded and unexamined commonsense, gives the air of truth to a literary product. In
a sense, the political scientist's excessive familiarity with

the subject matter has made him seek in descriptive wealth a substitute for butchering reality and reconstituting it in a drastically simplified model. This may account for the surprising power of the work of Anthony Downs in the face of its lack of political sophistication. The bare-bones logical model of the free market is remote from the rich actuality of existing markets, but it is a logical mechanism of great explanatory power where it applies. The success of the economists, such as it is, stems from their rigorous concentration on the creation of explanatory mechanisms, making these explicit and developing indicators by which their usefulness can be determined. Political scientists believe things about the separation of powers, party systems, and other political phenomena. The reasons that they find these beliefs logically compelling are, in logic at least, mostly rather simple. In all probability, parsimoniously stated, they would not require more verbiage than an economist's account of the market. Political scientists, however, have not concentrated on disentangling the logical reasons for their beliefs or those of political practitioners. Thus their beliefs, the explanations they find persuasive, have remained largely unarticulated. That which could—indeed, must—constitute the very beginning of significant theory has remained as shrouded in detail and complexity as the logic of a novel. The reader is carried by the rhetoric of plausibility. One may prefer Dostoevski to psychology, but with all its lack as literature, psychology has the merit of articulating its hypotheses for test. It is the merit of the present essay to focus on the critical importance of the logical explanatory mechanisms of social science. Their articulation and examination are conditions precedent to fruitful progress.

NORTON E. LONG

ACKNOWLEDGMENTS

I am grateful for the assistance provided under the terms of AID Contract #824 while I was working on the paradigm. Intellectually, my principal debts are to two of my colleagues. Stephen Toulmin, during the course of a joint seminar on comparative methodology of the physical and social sciences, did much to clarify my ideas about the problems discussed in the essay. And Norton Long has contributed so much to my thinking during a continuing dialogue that extends back to my arrival at Brandeis that I scarcely know where my ideas begin and his come to an end. Happily it does not matter, for he is the least inclined of anyone I know to construe his ideas as private possessions. *Rara avis.* Various others, notably Kenneth Waltz, read the manuscript in various stages of incompleteness and offered useful comments and assistance. None of these persons is in any way responsible for errors of fact, logic, or judgment.

December, 1967   E. J. M.

TABLE OF CONTENTS

CHAPTER ONE

EXPLANATION

IN recent years, interest in methodological questions has grown very rapidly in the social sciences, if not so spectacularly as interest in techniques and methods. In the search for guidelines to be used in the conduct of inquiry and the evaluation of claims to know, social scientists have for the most part relied upon one of two distinct and not wholly compatible traditions: the first, exemplified by the work of sociologists like Emile Durkheim or Robert K. Merton and anthropologists like Bronislaw Malinowski and A. R. Radcliffe-Brown, originated almost completely within the social sciences; the second, best exemplified by contemporary philosophy of science, has its origins in modern analytic philosophy, and particularly in logical empiricism. Without trying to choose between them, or even to select what is valuable in each, we find that they are in agreement on one fundamental point— that the goal of inquiry is explanation. Social scientists may disagree strongly about the role of evaluation or normative judgment in inquiry, about the criteria that an explanation must meet, or about the way in which explanation is best achieved; but the search for explanations, and for the descriptions on which explanations depend, is widely accepted as the prime goal of systematic inquiry.

The thesis to be defended in this essay is that neither the social science tradition nor the philosophy of science provides an adequate account of the explanatory process —another conception of explanation is required. The argument is directed primarily at the deductive paradigm of explanation currently accepted by most philosophers of science, partly because the methodological principles developed within the social sciences have already been subjected to telling criticism so often that nothing would be gained by adding to the indictment, but mainly because the deductive paradigm of explanation is implicit in most discussions of explanation in social science. The fact is that the deductive paradigm of explanation has been almost immune to criticism by social scientists, and is only rarely criticized by physical scientists or philosophers of science. A small group of traditionalists in social science have attacked *all* efforts to systematize social inquiry but the arguments employed are for the most part irrelevant because the whole notion of seeking for explanations is rejected.[1] In most instances, the deductive paradigm of explanation has been disseminated freely among social scientists, in implicit as well as explicit form, and accepted rather uncritically.

If the deductive paradigm of explanation is accepted as the standard, the explanatory capacity of the social sciences is extremely limited. While this has long been recognized, the limitations have usually been taken as a

[1]See my *Contemporary Political Thought: A Critical Study* (Dorsey Press, 1967), Ch. 2.

sign of the weakness of social science rather than as an indication of the limited usefulness of the deductive paradigm. Perhaps the major reason for taking that position has been the assumed adequacy of the deductive paradigm as an account of the mode of inquiry actually pursued in physical science. The reasoning runs as follows: physical science has been successful; its success has been due to the strength of its explanations; its explanations are strong because they are deductive in form; other disciplines can be equally successful only if they can meet the same explanatory requirements. This line of reasoning elevates the deductive paradigm into a privileged position in the conduct of inquiry—where it becomes an albatross around the neck of the social scientist. For social science simply cannot meet the requirements for deductive explanations. We do not have, and we are unlikely to get, the "nomic empirical generalizations" or "empirical laws" that deductive explanations demand. It follows, if the deductive paradigm is accepted, that the social scientist's capacity to explain is severely restricted and is likely to remain so for the indefinite future.

The dilemma seems unresolvable until we realize that it depends on a set of hidden assumptions that are not necessarily valid. If the term "explanation" *must* be defined as it appears in the deductive paradigm—if no alternative definition is possible—the argument holds. Further, if the kind of activity that has led the physical sciences to success is truly defined by the deductive paradigm, and no other conceptualization will fit the practices of the scientists, then the conclusion that science is successful *because* its explanations fit the deductive pattern may not be a *non sequitur*. Both of these assumptions can be challenged; indeed they are challenged here. Explanation *can* be defined in another way, and that definition fits the scientific enterprise as well as, if not better than, the deductive pattern. And, since it can be shown that an alternative definition of explanation is much more useful to the social (and physical) scientist, there are good reasons for preferring the alternative.

All definitions are open to modification, certainly, but the assertion that the deductive paradigm of explanation incorporates a serious misconstruction of scientific activity requires justification. The crux of the argument is that philosophers of science have defined "explanation" mainly in terms of logical properties of scientific theories and their definition ignores other aspects of scientific inquiry —particularly the purposes of inquiry and the use made of scientific theories and explanation—that are just as important as the logical characteristics of scientific explanations. The deductive paradigm assumes that scientists search for general laws that will "cover" particular cases. But the search for "laws of nature" seems part of the rhetoric of science; it has little relevance to scientific practice. What scientists actually do in their work can be construed in other ways. For example, the conception of scientific inquiry adopted here asserts that scientists seek intellectual instruments that permit understanding and control of the phenomena—that *control* is the central factor in the scientific enterprise. This conception is not wholly compatible with the deductive paradigm, for the emphasis on use and purpose (to control events) that follows from it leads to criteria of adequacy that cannot be met when the deductive paradigm is used. Those criteria can be satisfied, however, by adopting a different paradigm of explanation—here called a *system* paradigm.

One major purpose of the essay, then, is to suggest an

alternative way of conceiving scientific inquiry and the results of scientific inquiry—to produce an alternative definition of the term "explanation." It can be shown that: first, the definition is fully compatible with scientific practice; second, it avoids some of the conceptual difficulties inherent in the deductive paradigm; third, it offers the social scientist a meaningful and useful conception of explanation that is far less constrictive than the conception implicit in the deductive paradigm. The proposal is tentative, as are all such efforts, but the system paradigm seems an enormous improvement over the deductive paradigm, more particularly in social science but also in physical science. Even if it does no more than stimulate discussion of the foundations of the methodology of the social sciences, however, it will have served a useful purpose.

One final point may be worth touching upon briefly. If the effect of the deductive paradigm of explanation is constricting, or if the paradigm is improperly construed, the physical scientists might be expected to make their own protests against it, yet they have not done so. Is silence a sign of approval? Actually, there are some signs of unrest within the sciences, but the reason why physical science has not been affected by the deductive paradigm to anything like the same extent as social science seems to lie in the past history of the two areas of inquiry. Social science has not undergone the kind of theoretical development that took place in physical science. Long before there were philosophers of science to define the meaning of "theory," the physical scientists had developed quite sophisticated and powerful theories. The meaning of "theory" was learned operationally, in the same way and at the same time as the student learned how to carry out his investigations. Some few physical scientists have been much concerned with methodological or "philosophical" problems, but abstract discussion of methodology has played little part in the development of the meaning of "theory" in science or in the training of scientists. In fact, the philosophy of science definition of explanation is a *post hoc* reconstruction of the work that the physical scientists had actually performed and the instruments they employed. Physical scientists still work pragmatically, in most cases, ignoring the formal properties of their explanations and the writings of philosophers of science. Questions like "What is a theory?" rarely excite discussion among scientists. They know quite well what the term means within their own working context and they have developed quite sophisticated criteria for evaluating proposed theories. The deductive paradigm of explanation has not aroused the ire of the scientists primarily because the scientists have ignored it.

CHAPTER TWO

THE MEANING OF "EXPLANATION"

Whation"? If the question is
intended to elicit information about the "real" meaning
of explanation, then it cannot be answered. All that we
can do is suggest different ways in which the term might
be used, and try to give reasons why one usage should
be preferred to another. In the case of "explanation," we
have the advantage, or disadvantage, of being able to
examine what has already been done in the physical
sciences, and particularly in physics, since they are usually
taken as a model for systematic inquiry. One reason for
commending a particular conception of the process of
explanation, therefore, is that it conforms well to what
has actually been done in physical science. There are,
however, other considerations that are also relevant—as
this chapter will attempt to demonstrate.

Discussions of the meaning of terms like "explanation"
or "theory" have a peculiar "open" quality, a hint of
circularity, that can be quite distressing to anyone looking for the precision and finality usually associated
(wrongly) with science and methodology. The reason for
the open texture of the discussion is that there is no way

to "begin at the beginning" and thereby to ground the meaning of terms in some immutable base. To study explanation as it occurs in science, a cut must be made into an ongoing enterprise, an activity that has no beginning and no end, properly speaking. Even if Locke's *tabula rasa* could be achieved, the result would not be satisfactory; if the slate were wiped clean, nothing could be said about anything—man would perforce be mute.

Every exploration of the process of systematic inquiry, of the structure and use of the human conceptual apparatus, must make use of that apparatus. The problems confronting the methodologist have been likened, most aptly, to the dilemmas facing anyone trying to rebuild a ship while at sea. The analogy is useful, not because it suggests that methodologists are always "at sea," but because it reminds us that some parts of the conceptual apparatus must be stabilized, taken as given, if other parts are to be explored, and because it implies the futility of seeking to annihilate the past and somehow found human knowledge on an entirely new base. We must rebuild the ship; we cannot exchange it for another. What is implied by these considerations is that our conception of explanation must be compatible with an evolutionary conception of human knowledge, and that the quality of an explanation cannot be a fixed and definite matter. Explanations are produced by modification and improved by restructuring, amendment, amplification, or clarification, not by radical re-creation. And in the last analysis, the use that is made of an explanation, the relation of the explanation to our experience, determines its quality. However good a design may look on the drawing board, the ship built to its specifications must float before the design can be considered adequate.

The deductive paradigm of explanation

The meaning of "explanation" within the framework provided by the deductive paradigm is deceptively simple. An event is explained when it can be related to an established "empirical generalization" or "general law" according to the canons of formal logic; generalizations in turn are explained when they can be deduced from sets of "higher" generalizations or theories. The structure is held together by the rules of formal logical inference. The elements of the structure, the empirical generalizations or laws, must be available *before* explanation is possible. If the relation is to be deductive, generalizations must take the form "all *A* is *B*," or in some few cases "*n* percent of *A* is *B*." Other forms of generalization are not amenable to deductive inference. The generalizations, in other words, are established independently of the explanation; they are subject to "empirical verification" or test.[2] The principal criteria of an explanation are logical; the meaning of "explanation" is conceived in logical terms. That is, perhaps, to be expected, since the deductive paradigm was developed mainly by logicians interested in the philosophy of science, or more precisely, in the "logic of explanation" within the physical sciences.

Two aspects of the definition of explanation on which the deductive paradigm is based are particularly impor-

[2]For examples of the deductive paradigm, see R. B. Braithwaite, *Scientific Explanation: A Study of the Function of Theory, Probability, and Law in Science* (Cambridge University Press, 1953); Carl G. Hempel, *Aspects of Scientific Explanation and Other Essays in the Philosophy of Science* (Free Press, 1965), especially Pt. IV; Ernest Nagel, *The Structure of Science: Problems in the Logic of Scientific Explanation* (Harcourt, Brace & World, 1961), especially Ch. 3, "The Deductive Pattern of Explanation."

tant for the social scientist: First, the paradigm collapses or merges the logical and the empirical aspects of explanation; second, the definition attaches no weight to the purposes for which explanations are sought or to the manner in which they are used. The constricting effects of these features of deductive explanations are particularly severe in social science, though even in physical science the fusion of the empirical and the logical creates a number of serious obstacles to an adequate account of the explanatory process.

The fusion of the logical and empirical aspects of explanation occurs through the concept "empirical generalization." The concept is taken for granted by most philosophers of science, but discussions of the implications of the merger of description and logic are not altogether clear. In Carl G. Hempel, for example, we find the following:

The remarks made in this section are but special illustrations of two broader principles in the theory of science: first, the separation of "pure description" and "hypothetical generalization and theory-construction" in empirical science is unwarranted; in the building of scientific knowledge, the two are inseparably linked.[3]

Now, it is perfectly sound to argue that description uninformed by theory is impossible, or that empirical data not organized by some explanatory structure are meaningless. But it does not follow that the empirical and the logical aspects of explanation need not be separated. And there are good reasons to believe that separation is essential. One of the most critical aspects of explanation is the justification of a connection between an empirical descrip-

[3]Hempel, *op. cit.*, p. 243.

tion and a logical structure, whatever the concept of explanation that is employed. Logic cannot be applied to empirical events without justification. When the fusion is made without a warrant, it becomes a hidden form of question-begging.

In the deductive paradigm, the empirical and the logical come together through the "empirical generalizations" used in explanation. In the system paradigm, the linkage is made between an empirical description and a complete logical system. The reason for making the change is to avoid the problem of induction—which is presently insoluble. If the term "empirical" refers to description or observation, and the term "general" refers to a proposition that is valid without reference to time or place, then no proposition can be both empirical and general. And the conceptual stumbling block cannot be avoided by concentrating on the validation or confirmation of empirical generalizations, as Karl R. Popper and others suggest. No amount of empirical testing could possibly establish a general proposition because it refers to the future as well as the past, to what has not been observed as well as what has been observed. The system paradigm cannot solve the induction problem but it can provide a way of avoiding it altogether without emasculating the explanation.

There are other reasons for separating the empirical and the logical aspects of explanation that should not be overlooked. Their merger or fusion tends to blur the distinction between logical competence and possession of field-relevant knowledge—knowledge of relations that have held in the past, of attempts at explanation already rejected, of explanations accepted in related fields, etc. The adequacy of an explanation cannot be judged solely on logical grounds; some measure of logical competence is needed, but field-relevant knowledge is also essential. Each type of competence plays a different role in explanation, raising its own problems and requiring its own criteria of judgment. The crucial problem, fitting empirical data and logical propositions, is not a question that logic alone can settle—statisticians who seek to solve the problem by formal techniques not to the contrary. Separation of logic and empirical evidence calls attention to the need for both kinds of knowledge and reduces the possibility that either might be ignored.

Finally, by defining explanation in logical terms and ignoring the purposes for which explanations are used, the deductive paradigm in effect produces a single-factor standard for explanation and eliminates the possibility of grading explanations according to their usefulness. All deductive explanations are of a single quality. If the purpose for which explanations are used is added to the evaluative schema, grading is not only possible but necessary. And reference to purpose can provide the criteria needed for grading. The usefulness of grading may not be apparent in a highly developed field like physics but in the social sciences, where all explanations are imperfect, the introduction of grading or evaluation is enormously helpful. Incompleteness is not necessarily a handicap, for example, if reliability can be tested against a stated purpose. Grading allows the social scientist to use explanations that are partial and incomplete, and even explanations that are known to contain erroneous premises. If the purpose for which the explanation is intended can be fulfilled by a given structure, then that structure provides an explanation for the event which is adequate for that purpose. The introduction of purpose or use into the criteria of explanation is beneficial to social science in other ways to be examined more fully below.

Although the limits or faults in the deductive paradigm have been underscored heavily in this discussion, the aim is to suggest the points at which it proves inadequate, particularly in social science, not to argue that it is "wrong." Such terms are out of place in this context. The system paradigm of explanation outlined below defines explanation in a way that seems more useful in social science and more accurate in physical science. The essay sets forth the reasons why it is commended to the reader. Some familiarity with the deductive paradigm is assumed, and much of the work done in philosophy of science can be transferred without change. But the similarities are sometimes deceptive, and in fact a major transformation in conceptualization is involved in the transition. The requirements of explanation are modified radically, and the questions to be asked of an explanation are quite different.

The remainder of this chapter is devoted to a definition of "explanation." While it is written with one eye on the physical sciences, the principal focus is the linkage that can be established between the processes by which man acquires knowledge, the purposes that knowledge serves, and the instruments that fulfill those purposes. The goal is a definition of an intellectual construction that can be extremely useful, indeed essential, in the quest for knowledge—whether in physical or social science. The importance of the structure that is here called a system lies in its use and not in the name that is attached to it. Even if it were decided, for some reason, that the term "explanation" ought not to be applied to systems, they would still be invaluable and necessary. I am arguing, in other words, that one of the major purposes in inquiry is the production of structures that will perform certain functions or fulfill certain purposes. There are good reasons for calling these structures "explanations," but the nomenclature is a matter of convenience and simplicity. What is needed is a clear definition of the goals of inquiry and some understanding of the kinds of instruments that are needed to achieve those goals.

The meaning of "knowledge"

Given two competing definitions of the meaning of a term, some wider framework is needed if the respective merits of the two definitions are to be argued. The relative value or usefulness of the deductive paradigm of explanation and the system paradigm cannot be argued on the basis of dictionary definitions. In the case of explanation, that wider framework is supplied by a theory of knowledge. By stipulating what is meant by "knowledge," and inferring from the stipulations the kinds of instruments that are needed to acquire knowledge, it becomes possible to give reasons why one definition of explanation (as an instrument for acquiring knowledge) is to be preferred to another. What follows, therefore, is an attempt to anchor the meaning of "explanation" by reference to man's search for knowledge—defined in terms of the human perceptive apparatus, cognitive processes, and human needs. The account is painfully brief and oversimplified but it should indicate some of the reasons why the system paradigm of explanation is to be preferred to the deductive paradigm, even in physical science.

Man is born with a set of receptors that link him in certain limited ways to the physical and social environment. The linkage can be augmented or amplified by the use of various scientific instruments but the basic characteristics of the perceptive apparatus serve as one of the ultimate limits on man's capacity to know. Information obtained through the receptors, whether embedded in a language or transmitted by some "natural" energy system, pours into a central nervous system of magnificent proportions, self-stimulating, able to store and retrieve much of the information it receives, and most important of all, capable of generating abstract concepts that can be used to order and relate information (perceptions) in ways that are useful, in fact essential, for human life. Taking the empiricist position that man cannot obtain information except through the receptor apparatus, the human condition sketched above can serve as a base point for discussing the meaning of knowledge.

Unlike the lower orders of living things, human beings are born with very little in the way of built-in responses to the environment. Recognition of significant events in the environment and the development of appropriate response patterns must not only be learned, but the very apparatus used to attain these ends must be created by man himself—it is not inherited. Past experience must in some manner be organized or patterned so that sets of perceptions can be identified and related to other sets of perceptions in ways that permit man to anticipate subsequent events. At the most fundamental level, knowledge is organized experience and the search for knowledge is a search for patterns of organization. The organization is always created and not discovered. At an absolute minimum, man must generate enough knowledge to ensure survival. Ideally, knowledge should be reliable, accurate, cumulatable, corrigible, communicable, and useful to man in his efforts to adapt himself to the environment and modify the environment for his own purposes. The tools available are the experience gained from perception and the innate capacity to generate organizing concepts.

Since the social and physical environment is enormously complex, and the human mind has been prolific in the development of concepts that can order and arrange man's perceptions of that environment, we cannot hope to adjudicate every possible case in which a claim to know is put forward. Nor can we hope to deal with all of the purposes that knowledge serves or the ways in which that service is performed. The discussion that follows is therefore restricted to the kinds of organization of experience that enable man to anticipate and control events that take place in the physical and social environment—what would usually be called scientific knowledge. Doubtless, knowledge can serve to enrich human life in many other ways, but for our purposes, conceptualization intended for those purposes can be omitted. Furthermore, a distinction can be made between knowledge that is *personal* to the individual, not verbalized, and therefore not cumulatable and transferable, except by emulation, and *public* knowledge, available in oral or written form, and open to anyone with suitable training. Although there is no reason to suppose that personal knowledge is in any way different in form from public knowledge, it is clear that the massive cumulations of knowledge needed for contemporary life must be public rather than private. What can be learned by simple emulation, or even at the mother's knee, is not enough. The main difficulty is that personal knowledge is not open to the kind of critical, analytic evaluation that makes possible the expansion and cumulation of reliable knowledge which is the goal of science.

Of course, there is a sense in which private knowledge, however acquired, can serve a useful purpose—even in scientific inquiry. For example, when empirical data are being fitted to a logical structure, judgments about the adequacy of fit, the aptness of the analogy, may bring personal knowledge into play. It is not merely that those who have conducted exhaustive studies into particular aspects of social life may possess public knowledge that has not yet been disseminated. The residue of private knowledge that remains when self-conscious verbalization has taken place may still be useful, particularly as a critical tool. Ultimately, the prime criterion of the adequacy of a claim to knowledge must be the available public knowledge in the field, but during the early stages of inquiry the potential uses of private knowledge ought not to be overlooked. An individual who has spent a lifetime in politics, for example, may be a gold mine of information if we can learn how to extract the gold and separate it from the dross in which it is usually embedded. There seems no good reason why this rather nebulous asset should not be employed whenever possible—with suitable precautions, of course.

Knowledge and purpose

If knowledge is organized human experience, the manner in which experience is organized (including the processes by which explanations are created or formulated) will depend on the operation of the perceptive and cognitive apparatus in man and on the purposes for which knowledge is needed and used. The perceptive and cognitive structures define the limits of the possible; human purposes determine the value and significance of what is possible. I am here adopting the point of view called instrumentalism, i.e., the belief that knowledge is only a tool or instrument, hence that it can be evaluated only in terms of its human uses—its value to man. The corollary to that position, which is called nominalism, asserts that the meaning of words lies in the conventions that define their use, and therefore denies that words can have any "essential" meaning, any "real" counterpart in the natural universe. From this point of view, claims to know cannot be judged against absolute truth or unvarying reality because man cannot assert on defensible grounds the existence of absolute truth or unvarying reality. The quality of knowledge depends on the purposes that it will serve.

A claim to know is therefore no more than an assertion to the effect that a particular way of organizing human experience is useful for a particular purpose. Without a statement of purpose, usefulness cannot be judged. There is no such thing as "usefulness in general." Use is related to a particular end. It follows that there can be no general procedures for organizing human experience (in effect, no general theories without specific referrants) and no general procedures for evaluating claims to know. Further, ways of organizing experience (explanations and theories) are neither true nor false since there can be no criteria for judging them so. Either they serve a given purpose or they do not (within the realm of scientific knowledge) and that is determined by pragmatic test. There are therefore no general explanations; all explanations must make reference to specific events and relate to specific purposes.

This underlines one of the major differences between the deductive paradigm of explanation and the system paradigm proposed here. Since the deductive paradigm makes no reference to purpose, it cannot state criteria for evaluating explanations. What is provided instead is a formal definition of an explanation. But if there are no general explanations, and no final or "true" explanations, then the search for "the" explanation, which is enforced by the mode of definition used in the deductive paradigm, is equally futile. Granted that philosophers of science have set the standard of explanation very high—so high that explanation in social science is virtually eliminated— the cost in flexibility is too great. Whatever the terminology ultimately adopted in social science, it is clear that there is much to be gained by evaluating the various structures that can be used to organize experience according to the purposes they serve rather than according to their correspondence to an overly strict definition of explanation. If the aim of inquiry is to acquire some measure of control over a particular event or set of events, then any instrument that will perform that function is useful and adequate, whatever it may be called. The desirability of adopting this conception of inquiry, argued more fully below, is greatly enhanced by its side effects, particularly the impetus it gives to examining the reasons why a specific inquiry is undertaken.

Anticipation and control of the environment

What purposes *can* knowledge, or organized experience, serve? Here I suggest that we define purpose in terms of two fundamental human needs or requirements: first, the need to *anticipate* future events so that behavior can be adapted to them; second, the need to be able to *control* future events (the past is beyond control) so that man can become something more than a servile prisoner of natural forces. Defining human needs in this way makes it possible to produce a definition of explanation that is not wholly arbitrary—that can be justified at least in part on empirical grounds. By defining human purposes in terms of these needs, purpose can be included in the criteria of explanation without excluding the possibility of a general treatment of the explanatory process, and without restricting the evaluation of particular explanations in terms of specific needs.

Whether man's purpose in inquiry is to anticipate what will occur in the environment, or to intervene in the environment in order to control or modify the course of events, he must have reliable expectations about the future if he is to succeed. But the two needs are analytically distinct, and the capacity to control the environment depends on an intellectual instrument that is much more complex than the instrument needed to provide anticipations alone. We can therefore distinguish the instruments by the needs they are capable of satisfying, or putting the matter another way, define the characteristics of the instrument according to the need it is intended to satisfy. Before an instrument will allow control over the environment, it must meet certain specifiable, minimum criteria.

Two other human "needs" that are sometimes alleged as purposes of inquiry are here specifically rejected. The "satisfaction of human curiosity" begs the question. Granting that curiosity is found in human beings, and that it demands satisfaction, it would still be necessary to stipulate the conditions under which curiosity *should be* satisfied. Otherwise, each person would have his own unique criteria of satisfaction and agreement on the content or meaning of knowledge would be impossible. Similarly, the human need for "understanding," highly touted by some social scientists as a goal of inquiry, is so grossly ambiguous that it is almost impossible to assign it a definite meaning. To the extent that the term means anything reasonably specific, to "understand" seems to imply possession of an explanatory instrument, an instrument that makes possible control over the environment. If the term means more than this, it remains for those who assert the claim to demonstrate its usefulness and the means by which it might be satisfied. Here, to "understand" means to be able to explain and no more.

Forecasts and explanations

Expectations about the future can be created in a variety of ways using a number of different instruments. For our purposes, the instruments capable of generating expectations can be divided into two classes: (1) *forecasts,* which may come from intuition, prophecy, statistical predictions, or hunches, and may be quite accurate, but which do not suggest ways in which man might intervene to control the events that are expected; (2) *explanations,* which also generate expectations about the future, but go beyond forecasts to provide us with understanding of past events and to suggest ways in which future events might in principle be controlled. The meaning of explanation is in this way linked to the human need to control events in the empirical world; an explanation is an instrument that suggests ways in which man might *in principle* intervene in an empirical situation to alter the course of events. Limiting the requirement to control "in principle" rather than in practice does not weaken the power of the explanation but acknowledges the relevance of the technology available at the time, of our actual capacity to control the environment. To accept an explanation as valid means to believe that if it could be acted upon, events could be controlled in particular ways. Since the quality of the instruments that might perform this function will obviously vary greatly, it will be necessary, in due course, to discuss the terms in which explanations can be evaluated (Chapter Five).

Both forecasts and explanations, then, generate expectations about future events. In explanations, and in forecasts based on statistical projections, expectations are produced by linking two or more sets of events according to stipulated rules. But an explanation carries the added requirement that a deliberate modification of the relations that generate those expectations will in principle produce a change of outcomes in the empirical world as well as in the logical structure in which the expectations originate. This eliminates the danger of accepting spurious correlations as an explanation for an event. For example, there is a known correlation between sunspot activity and economic cycles in the United States. Even granting that the degree of correlation is so high between the events that one can serve as a predictor for the other, the prediction will result from a forecast and not an explanation unless it can be argued that a change in the economic cycle in the United States would induce a change in sunspot activity on the sun, or conversely that a major change in sunspot activity would be followed by a change in economic activity in the United States. At the moment that seems most unlikely unless the indicators are so loosely defined that the structure is beyond test.

The use of forecasting devices that can predict future events quite accurately is so widely known that the possibility of creating them requires no argument. Is it possible, however, to create instruments that can satisfy the requirements of an explanation as defined above? The instrument must not only predict but provide control in principle over events. Control over events in turn depends on our capacity to specify "how" or "why" events occur, since knowledge of the way in which events come about makes it possible to intervene, in principle at least, to control them. Knowing that the processes that result in deadly mosquitoes involve the development of eggs in stagnant pools of water, intervening by covering the surface of the water with oil and thus cutting off the supply of oxygen to the eggs, will in principle inhibit their growth—providing that the effect of oxygen deprivation on eggs is known. If an instrument can be created that will specify the sets of interactions that are linked empirically with the event to be explained or controlled, explanation in terms of our definition is possible.

To provide an explanation, then, an event must be embedded in a set of relationships, tied to other events, so that observation of part of the set of interactions leads to justified expectations about the remainder. Control over the event can in principle be achieved by manipulation of the relations specified in the explanation. An explanation of precipitation, for example, is attained by creating a structured set of relations in which precipitation is linked to other elements in the environment—air, temperature, humidity, etc. The connection is made by stating the rules by which the variables or elements interact in such manner that one of the consequences of the interactions is precipitation. Control over precipitation can in principle be attained by altering the relevant variables in the situation. Intervention in the environment in the requisite way may be a practical impossibility, but if the explanation is to be considered adequate there must be some reason to believe that a drastic reduction in air temperature, other factors remaining equal, would lead to precipitation if there were enough moisture in the air. The explanation is logical to the extent that it generates expectations about the consequences of specified interactions among stipulated variables. The process is empirical to the extent that the interactions must have an observational base and the consequences of interaction must be relevant to some concrete empirical situation.

As a first approximation, an explanation is defined as a way of organizing human experience to show how or why events occur by linking those events to other events according to stipulated rules. The logical calculations possible within the structure provide the warrant for expecting particular events to occur under specified conditions and at the same time provide the possibility of control in principle over the event through manipulation of the variables. The quality of the explanation can be evaluated in terms of the purposes for which it is used. A weak explanation provides minimal control over a limited part of the environment, control that may be in various degrees unreliable; a strong explanation provides accurate and reliable control over substantial parts of the environment. The scope, power, reliability, and usefulness of an explanation can vary greatly, and each explanation must be evaluated separately in terms of specific purposes.

An illustration will clarify the distinction between an explanation and a forecast and suggest the utility of the proposed definition of explanation. It is a commonplace that a variety of techniques can produce quite accurate forecasts of, say, the number of traffic deaths to be expected in the United States in a given year. For some purposes, such as estimating the number of coffins that will be filled in that year, a forecast is all that is needed. In general, forecasts will suffice in all cases where man's aim is to adapt himself to the environment rather than seek to control it for his own purposes—a fatalistic attitude in keeping with the tone of the illustration. But if the number of traffic deaths is a source of concern, if it has normative or evaluative significance, and we wish to control it rather than adapt to it, then a forecast is no more than an indication of the size of the problem. It suggests nothing about the way in which traffic deaths might be controlled or reduced. In general, the demand for an explanation arises out of a normative judgment; the explanatory apparatus rests on a normative base. The exception occurs in highly developed fields like physics where explanations of particular events are required on theoretical rather than utilitarian grounds.

Common sense suggests that we cannot control the number of traffic deaths that will occur in any given year unless we know how or why traffic deaths occur, and in this case common sense is an excellent guide. Given knowledge of the way in which traffic deaths occur, of the factors that enter into traffic accidents, and the rules governing the interactions of those factors, it is possible to explain particular traffic deaths; by increasing the number of explanations, all or most traffic deaths can be explained, though complete explanation of a class of events defined with reference to some other criterion than the explanatory structure is not essential for successful intervention. We may be able to explain only a part of the total number of traffic deaths in society, but those that can be explained are in principle subject to control. Some deaths, for example, can be explained by reference to intoxication, others to mechanical failures in vehicles, road and weather conditions, and so on. There is no need to seek for a single explanation for the whole class of events that we call traffic deaths; the class was defined prior to the explanation, and no explanation can deal with events not defined by its own terms of reference. If an explanation can be found for the entire class, well and good, but explanations for portions of the total can always be used to deal with some part of the class of events for which an explanation is sought. These partial explanations will suggest that reduction of accidents may be achieved by reducing the incidence of driving under the influence of intoxicants, by discouraging driving in bad weather, or by improving the quality of the highways. The accuracy of the explanations may vary, and the precise amount of reduction in traffic deaths that can be achieved by using them will have to be determined pragmatically, but it seems clear that some use can be had from a fairly simple set of explanations, readily produced from information already available. In due course, these explanations may be rendered more precise, and perhaps amalgamated into a single structure that will deal with the entire class.

The commonplace nature of the example, and the rather trivial character of the explanations, may seem out of keeping with the abstract tone of the essay, but it was in fact deliberately chosen to illustrate the kinds of explanations that social science is already able to make in terms of the system paradigm. Such explanations are useful; in fact, we could hardly build societies without them. So long as their limitations are recognized and they are not used for purposes for which they are inadequate, it seems needlessly pedantic to insist that they are not explanations because they do not involve relating a particular event or class of events to an empirical generalization. For some purposes, they will do.

The example also illustrates the value of including the requirement for control in principle over events in the

definition of explanation. Given the definition, any intellectual construction that can satisfy its terms will serve
some useful purpose. Further, given the definition, a great
deal can be said about the kind of instrument that is
needed to fulfill its terms. As we shall see below, a powerful explanation performs almost identical functions whether it is clothed in the conceptual garb of the deductive
paradigm or explicated in terms of the system paradigm.
The usefulness of the system paradigm begins to emerge
when powerful explanations are not available, for it demonstrates the potential utility of weaker members of the
explanatory family. For the social scientist, the development and use of weak explanations is a matter of great
importance since all of his explanations are likely to be
weak. The only additional burden involved in the use of
the system paradigm is the need for criteria for evaluating
the quality of an explanation—and they are readily supplied by considering the purpose that the explanation is
to serve.

The system paradigm, in other words, suggests the desirability of making a beginning, however rough, at explaining particular events. Quality can then be improved
by modification and amendment; experience allows us to
fit an explanation more closely to experience. The initial
construction may be badly designed, the variables included in the system ill-chosen, the rules of interaction grossly
imperfect; further inquiry may even lead us to destroy the
original structure and begin anew. But if the conception
of inquiry remains constant, something will be learned,
even from failure. The social sciences have too long been
plagued by practitioners who demanded that their intellectual heritage be razed to the ground in the name of
some "new" approach—usually derived from the ancient

Greeks. In part this is a consequence of the tendency among social scientists to emphasize an "approach" rather than the explanation of concrete, singular events. On the whole, social scientists are identified by their approach rather than by their interest in a particular kind of phenomenon, though there are signs of change in the air. It seems clear that it is highly desirable to begin systematic inquiry with concrete cases, chosen on normative grounds, or in some few cases, because of their theoretical relevance. Once the kinds of events that need explanation are agreed on, a determined effort to explain them can lead to cumulation of theory rather than isolated and sporadic attempts at theory construction. The aim of science may well be explanation, but Marx was at least partly correct—to seek explanations without some intentions with respect to the events to be explained is a curious kind of activity that is exceptionally difficult to justify.

The difference in outlook implied by the use of the system paradigm of explanation rather than the deductive paradigm can perhaps be suggested by considering the philosopher's favorite, the deductive explanation of the whiteness of a European swan. According to those who accept the deductive paradigm, the question, "Why is that swan white?" can be answered, in Europe, by referring the questioner to the "established empirical generalization" which states that "All European swans are white," and to the rules of formal logic. The swan's color is explained by showing that the observed color can be deduced from the generalization. Anyone using the system paradigm would first of all want to know, "What is your purpose in asking?" Because the deductive paradigm avoids the question, the explanations it provides may tell us nothing that is in any sense useful, except to keep small children from asking further questions. The deductive paradigm provides no basis for discriminating between an explanation of a significant event and a logician's exercise. That distinction may be trivial for the logician but it is extremely important to anyone engaged in empirical inquiry. And it is worth noting that an explanation of the swan's color offered by a physical scientist, making use of genetic theory, optical theory, etc., would satisfy precisely the criteria of explanation that we have proposed. In fact, there seems no exception to the rule that explanations accepted within physical science *do* provide control in principle over events. And discussion of the problem with working scientists supports the view that what the scientist seeks with his theories *is* control over events. At the very least, these considerations suggest that it would be a serious error to ignore the role of purpose in inquiry when criteria of explanation are being discussed.

CHAPTER THREE

THE STRUCTURE OF EXPLANATIONS

REASONED and intentional control over the environment, as distinguished from activity that may influence the environment in unpredictable ways, requires a way of structuring the relations among events that will allow the user to foresee with some confidence the consequences of altering those relations. The instrument that makes this possible is the *system*. Systems are formal logical structures, sets of variables and the rules governing their interactions. One of the basic elements in any explanation, therefore, will be a system. However, since explanations must have objects, must be relevant to something in human experience, each explanation will also involve a *description* which contains the events to be explained. Construed as a process, explanation is the application of a logical system to a description.

An explanation has been defined as an instrument that will tell us how or why an event occurs in the empirical world, thereby making it possible in principle to control that event. I have tried to indicate some of the reasons why it is useful to define explanation in that way. It remains now to examine in more detail the properties of systems and descriptions that make explanation a practical possibility. The characteristics of a good explanation are illustrated by a well-established example from physical science, couched in terms of the system paradigm rather than the deductive paradigm. In subsequent chapters, the explanatory process is examined under the more difficult conditions normal in social science, that is, when the explanation proposed for an event has not been established and its quality is unknown.

DESCRIPTION

Description begins, necessarily, with perception. Perception belongs to the past. Hence description can only assert what man has already experienced, not what he might have experienced or what he will in the future experience. Nothing in the canons of logic permits a deductive inference from observed experience to either the unexperienced past or to the future—that is the crux of the induction problem. So much is commonplace, though it suffices to invalidate the use of the concept "empirical generalization" in inquiry.

Explanation does, however, require the use of general or timeless statements, since expectations are possible in the future only if propositions made in the present can in some fashion be extended into the future, or more precisely, carried into the future with confidence. In the deductive paradigm, the extension is allegedly based on the process of induction, and some philosophers claim that it is possible to construct a logic of induction that will hold for that process. In the system paradigm, timeless or general propositions are assumed to belong to the logical rather than the empirical world. They may be used to create expectations about the empirical world only if there is some warrant or justification for assuming isomorphism between an empirical situation and the logical structure of a system. The difference between this way of construing general propositions and the way in which they are conceived in the deductive paradigm may seem trivial but it avoids a great deal of conceptual complication. There is no need, in the system paradigm, to ask for *empirical* statements that hold into eternity. Instead, we ask under what circumstances we can expect a given set of relations to hold with reference to empirical data. The empirical and logical components of explanation are kept distinct, but if they can be related (in ways to be discussed below), implications derived from the logical structure can be transferred to the empirical world with results that either justify or invalidate the transfer. The introduction of purpose into the defining criteria of an explanation provides the means for justifying such transfers, since the reason for making the transfer is to fulfill the purpose of the inquiry. Pragmatic success, coupled with various other criteria that can be applied to the explanatory process, provides an adequate, if problematic, indicator of the validity or the warrant for using a given explanation in a particular case. A brief sketch of the salient features of an empirical description will suggest some of the reasons for approaching the problem of explanation in this way.

As David Hume pointed out long ago, human perceptions are discrete and singular; the relations or connections among perceptions must be supplied by man. The apparatus that serves to connect our perceptions is neither true nor false, for there are no criteria by which truth or falsity could be judged; it can only be more or less useful for a stipulated purpose. The fundamental goal of a description, then, is to pattern or organize perceptions in ways that are useful and not in ways that are true. In other words, descriptions are required if explanations are to be offered for events within those descriptions. The problem is complicated, however, by the fact that the structures used to organize perceptions are so deeply embedded in the language that they are learned unconsciously, for the most part, with the language. Even the simplest of geometric figures is an abstract classification scheme that we must learn to recognize; it is never a "natural" aggregate of perceptions. It follows that the way perceptions are organized in practice depends very much on the implicit structuring of perceptions carried out by the language. That is the point that so much concerned Karl Mannheim and others interested in "the sociology of knowledge." The consequences of the situation are not so serious as Mannheim seemed to believe, though they complicate the process of inquiry, particularly in social science. Given self-conscious recognition of the problem, it has proved possible to generate concepts, and descriptions based on those concepts, that are notably "culture free," i.e., free from the influence of the implicit structuring of a given language. There is no reason in principle why the same results cannot be obtained in social science, though it may require more conscious attention by the social scientist than by the physical scientist.

One implication of this characteristic of human thought is worth stressing. No explanation can be concerned with *the* facts, or with *the* empirical situation. Any set of perceptions can be ordered in an infinite number of different ways, hence any description is no more than one way of ordering them. Explanations cannot simply fit *the* description, for an explanation can be made to fit almost any set of facts. Explanations fit *a* description, and that description depends on the terms in which the explanation is formulated. That is the reason why an explanation will hold only for the class of events defined by the fundamental terms of the explanation; classes of empirical perceptions devised for other purposes may not be amenable to explanation by a single structure—as we saw in the case of automobile accidents. For that reason, explanation should focus on the single event, particularly in the early stages of its development, rather than on a predefined class.

Concepts

A description is an organization of perceptions. At an absolute minimum, "organization" implies the application of a rule or set of rules to a collection of entities; the rules used to organize human perceptions are called *concepts*. They are human creations, not natural entities, and without them man could hardly be said to think. Concepts serve to identify the entities we think about, classify entities into related sets, relate entities in time and space, define attributes, and perform all of the other functions implied in the term "organization of experience." All languages contain concepts, of course, though not all of the concepts in a language are useful in description. The total supply of concepts in a language, or in an academic discipline, fluctuates constantly as old concepts disappear, new concepts are invented, or modifications of various sorts are introduced into the conceptual apparatus.

One of the major tasks in theory, whatever the discipline, is the clarification, modification, or invention of concepts, and some of the major headaches in theory stem from inadequacies, often unrecognized, in the conceptual armory. Confucius' demand for a "rectification of terms," though not precisely parallel to present-day problems of conceptualization, is a useful reminder of the time that has elapsed since man first became aware of his conceptual problems, and an indication of the unlikelihood that all of man's conceptual problems will be completely solved.

The usefulness of a concept is field-dependent, but certain kinds of conceptual inadequacies are recurrent, particularly in the social sciences. The worst sin in conceptualization, certainly, is ambiguity. Since concepts are rules that organize or relate perceptions, ambiguity in the rules will produce a blurred, undependable description and uncertain or unreliable communication. Concepts must define unambiguously a specified set of perceptions and exclude all others as rigorously as possible, particularly if they are to be used in description. Otherwise, the concepts are not defeasible, leading to endless, nonintersecting arguments—as with terms like "democracy" or "equality." Propositions that include ambiguous concepts are untestable by observation, hence indeterminate. The extreme of ambiguity, the concept that has *no* empirical referents yet is used in description, still appears occasionally, even in social science, though medieval scholasticism is the classic illustration of the human capacity to build elaborate arguments about what is alleged to be the case by agreeing on the use of concepts in sentences without agreeing about the empirical indicators to which those concepts refer. Freudian psychiatry suffered from the same disease. Every language includes some terms that have no empirical referents, but propositions that claim to assert what is the case (describe) must include at least *some* concepts that are tied unambiguously to specified observations if they are to be judged true or false (propositions about empirical observations may be true or false even though the content of the proposition is not true or false relative to the external world). Empiricism, in other words, is a necessary condition for systematic inquiry—though it is not and cannot be a sufficient condition for science.

Unlike conceptual ambiguity, conceptual vagueness can be useful and even highly desirable. Every explanation makes use of some concepts (theoretical terms) that cannot be defined completely in terms of observations. And the heuristic value of structures that are not explanations is often much enhanced by the use of vague concepts. "Anxiety," for example, is distressingly vague and woolly in current usage; it is very difficult to say with any confidence whether or not a given person is anxious. But it has called attention to an aspect of human behavior that might easily be overlooked if all of the concepts used in social inquiry were defined fully in empirical terms. When new dimensions are being added to inquiry (new concepts are being introduced), vagueness is to be expected, and it may be advantageous. In time, of course, concepts should become more precisely defined if they are to be retained and used.

The usefulness of a concept depends almost entirely on the purpose of inquiry. However precisely it may be defined, the concept "farmer" will be far too loose for a study of the life styles of American citizens since it includes persons who are millionaires as well as paupers. Even an advertising agency preparing a list of customers for a farm equipment manufacturer may still choose to subdivide the class "farmers" according to income, thus saving some advertising expense. Concepts, in a word, are acceptable because of their definitions and useful because of the purposes they serve.

The concepts used in social science are largely adaptations from everyday speech and common usage, and both vagueness and ambiguity are common. Should the social sciences follow physical science into standardization of concepts—develop a technical language? The case for standardization has been urged quite frequently, and most social scientists would probably agree that some measure of standardization would be useful, but there are both practical and theoretical problems of considerable difficulty that would have to be solved first. For one thing, the machinery needed to enforce standardization of concepts in social science simply does not exist; commitment to particular usage is today a personal decision and not a community decision. In practical terms, standardization is most unlikely in the foreseeable future.

The more interesting and tendentious question, however, is whether standardization is really desirable—whether it ought to be pursued as a goal. At a minimum, the use of standardized concepts implies some commitment to the study of specific classes of events within a broadly defined conceptual framework. Social science has no structure of this kind at present, and social scientists are usually identified by the department that employs them rather than by the conceptual framework they employ or the phenomena they investigate. Is a change desirable? It is worth noting that the cure could be worse than the disease. The chief difficulty is the need to decide on the concepts and framework that will serve as a base for standardization. Concepts organize perceptions by linking them together into classes, but concepts also organize by exclusion. Standardized concepts would therefore exclude broad ranges of perceptions from consideration, and in an undeveloped discipline, the significance of what is excluded would be impossible to assess. Further, the use of standard concepts, given the structure of university training, could too easily lead to ossification and it may be more important to keep open the possibility of reconceptualizing the field than to reap the benefits of standardization. Significantly, in this context, most of the great advances in science have been contingent upon a major restructuring of the conceptual apparatus employed in a field and not on the acquisition of "new" facts. The more limited the discipline, the less likely it becomes that adequate reasons could be given for closing the conceptual apparatus in a particular way. Suggestions to the effect that social scientists should employ a particular set of concepts in their work are clearly premature at this point; gradual or tentative standardization seems the only sensible way to proceed given the circumstances.

The elements of a description

For our purposes, descriptions will be taken to consist of two basic types of concepts or sets of concepts, although others will be needed to complete the requirements of the language in which the description appears. *Classifications* organize perceptions into entities; they define the properties of the things about which we think. *Relational propositions* connect classifications or relate them by recording simultaneous or successive variations in the composition of a set of classifications, or by recording variations in the values of the individual variables in the set included in the description. Relational propositions are *not* generalizations; they are merely records of past observations. Various kinds of relational propositions may be used in description: the variables in a set may simply be enumerated; changes in the values of the variables in a set may be recorded over time; or changes in the composition of a set of variables may be recorded over time. In the first case, the description is *static;* when the description records change, it is *dynamic.* In all cases, relational propositions link a particular value of one or more variables to a particular value in other variables in the set; they cannot state "general rules" linking changes in sets of values over time. For example, boiling can be linked to a particular water temperature, but a general relational statement like "water boils at 212° F." is not a description. The verb in a description is always in the past tense.

It is useful to distinguish between a description that records a *difference* between two or more things and a description that contains a record of *change.* Differences make description possible, for a world in which everything was the same could not be described. Change, on the other hand, is a difference that appears over time. It is possible to have a world in which differences remain unchanged, though not a world in which there are changes but no differences. Only change requires explanation. Differences simply *are;* they are beyond explanation unless the differences that now are did not exist at some other time. Today's differences may be explained if they did not hold yesterday; e.g., the geologist can explain why a mountain appears today where no mountain appeared ages ago even though the mountain remained unchanged in his lifetime. The importance of the distinction between change and difference appears when the adequacy of a description is being evaluated, when we begin to explain. The description that contains the event to be explained must hold a record of change, else no explanation is possible. The event to be explained will *be* a change and not merely a difference. Descriptions, in other words, must be dynamic and not static if they are to be used in explanation.

The quality of a description will depend, obviously, on the concepts it employs and on the accuracy of the observations it embodies. Concepts should be linked firmly to observations; observations should be measured as precisely as possible. Other things equal, the higher the quality of the scale used to measure, the better the description; a description couched in terms of an interval scale is to be preferred to a description scaled on an ordinal scale. Since the quality of the explanation applied to the description depends directly on the quality of the description, precision of measurement is a highly desirable feature in descriptions—provided, of course, that significance is not sacrificed to precision.

A less obvious aspect of description that should be considered when it is being evaluated is the kind of conceptual framework employed by the inquirer. Without a conceptual framework, a theoretical structure that can assign significance to different perceptions, description is impossible. There are no "natural" or neutral descriptions. A faulty conceptual structure can lead to hopeless bias in the description and hinder or even prevent explanation. The conceptual framework, the linked set of concepts that serves as a selecting mechanism for the observer, functions in the same way that spectacles serve the man who is blind without them. What is seen depends on the characteristics of the spectacles rather than the characteristics of the "reality" viewed through the spectacles. The facts do not lie before the observer, immutable and unchangeable. What a fact *is* depends on the conceptual framework through which perceptions are screened.

Events and phenomena

Since a description is an organized *selection* of perceptions, and the rules of selection are determined by the conceptual framework, the structure of the conceptual framework determines which events in the environment appear significant, stand out from the background. Such outstanding events we will call *phenomena*. Phenomena are the events for which explanations are sought; they serve as the focal point for systematic inquiry. Since they are derived from the conceptual framework, a change in conceptualization will have an enormous impact on the aims and purposes of inquiry. For example, a botanist and a zoologist may have the same set of perceptions, say by walking through the same field, but they "see" quite different phenomena—they order perceptions differently. In fact, what identifies the two men as botanist and zoologist respectively is the fact that they make use of different, identifiable conceptual frameworks. For that reason, each will give a different account of the phenomena in the field, and the descriptions that they provide of the events in the field may differ radically. It follows that the results obtained from their work will have different uses and may be of different quality. The same distinctions appear *within* a discipline, of course; a student of kinship relations and a student of political institutions will not see the same phenomena even though they examine the same village.

The example provides a good illustration of the way in which the theoretical and the empirical aspects of inquiry intermingle and overlap. The conceptual framework used in inquiry must be suitable to the descriptive situation; if the concepts included in the framework are not matched by the perceptions included in the description, the apparatus is useless. On the other hand, the events to be studied must appear in some conceptual framework else they could not be identified as events. Circularity is avoided if the connection between description and theoretical structure is construed as a reciprocal and not an undirectional relation. Ultimately, the observer must assume that the observations refer to something external to himself that can serve as a check on the viability of the conceptual apparatus. Every empiricist, like it or not, must assume there is "something out there" that he cannot describe fully or "really," but that he cannot change either —empiricists must be "naturalists." Otherwise, no set of perceptions could break the circularity of the relation and allow one element in the relation to serve as arbiter over the other. When conceptual apparatus and observation conflict, the framework, not the observation, ultimately must give way. The question of when an established conceptual framework should be abandoned is one of the more difficult problems of inquiry, and even in the physical sciences one may be maintained persistently in the face of considerable evidence of inadequacy—opposition to geological interpretations of the age of the earth, or to the Darwinian account of the development of man, is a good illustration of the point.

Description and purpose

The importance of purpose in the evaluation of explanations has already been stressed and will be considered further below. The need to specify purpose before adequate descriptions can be produced is less commonly realized yet equally important. Since there can be no absolute description or "true" description, no description will serve all purposes. In the absence of a statement of purpose, the adequacy of a description is indeterminate. An example will make the point best in this case.

Assume that two observers (O_1 and O_2) follow a driver (D) as he moves down the main thoroughfare in a large city. Each is asked to describe D's behavior when another vehicle approaches and he must either yield or seize the right-of-way. Even if the focus of the description is agreed, the observer is faced with the hopeless task of selecting the factors that should be included in his description. If he records the fact that another vehicle approached n times and D yielded the right-of-way $n - a$ times and seized the right-of-way in all other cases he will have done everything possible, given the terms of his mandate. If the mandate suggested that the observer include all significant factors, but failed to identify a reference point for assessing significance, the observer is almost bound to fail to provide an adequate description. Assume, for example, that O_1 records the direction from which other vehicles approach and the time remaining before D is due at his office while O_2 records, for whatever reason, the size of the other vehicle and the sex of its driver. Both descriptions are incomplete, of course, but since all descriptions are incomplete, that is not the central problem in the example. Assuming that both descriptions are accurate, are they in any sense "adequate"?

It is clear that there are some purposes which the two descriptions, taken alone or together, cannot serve. An insurance investigator who wishes to know whether or not D is a good insurance risk would want information not included in either description. If the inquiry was meant to determine whether or not drivers in the city were following the legal maxim, "Cede the right-of-way to the vehicle on the right in all cases," some of the information would be unnecessary. If we wished to know how accurately D perceived the situation before him, neither description will do. The "simple" process of description is not at all simple in practice.

Let us introduce one final complication. Assume that D actually followed the following rule while driving: "Cede the right-of-way to all larger vehicles and to all women drivers; seize the right-of-way in all other cases." Leaving aside the survival value of the rule, and assuming that D will always perceive the situation correctly, does it follow that no explanation of D's behavior would be possible unless the description included the information required by the rule that D actually followed? Curiously enough, that is not the case. It would be possible, for example, using psychological concepts, to produce an explanation of his driving behavior that made no reference to the terms of D's actual rule of driving, yet accounted for his behavior quite adequately. The description of D's behavior would make use of exactly the same set of perceptions, but they would be organized on different principles —around different concepts.

It is often said that the aim of inquiry is to describe, explain, or evaluate, and the implication sometimes assumed is that these three goals are both logically and functionally separate and independent. Our discussion of description, hopefully, demonstrates the impossibility of making the separation in other than analytic terms. Uninformed accumulation of descriptive data is meaningless. The Baconian approach to inquiry involves not merely one fallacy but two: explanations cannot be derived from collections of facts, however large, hence fact collecting has no intrinsic value; furthermore, the facts cannot even be collected until some criteria of relevance are available.

EXPLANATION

Explanations, according to the definition proposed in the previous chapter, must provide understanding of the past, generate expectations relevant to the future, and suggest ways in which man can in principle intervene to alter or control events. Every explanation must have an object, an event to be explained—a phenomenon. Since explanation cannot deal with all of the past, or all events in the future, the phenomenon must be specific and limited. But it is not enough to select an isolated event for explanation, for no event can be explained in isolation. Events must be embedded in an empirical situation, lodged in a description containing other events and relational statements linking the two. Descriptions must contain networks of interrelated events before explanation is possible.

The reason is simple enough. No event can generate expectations about itself; something external to the event to be explained must trigger our expectations. We do not "expect to see an event" in isolation; some event in the past or future must be connected to other events in ways that lead us to expect one when the other is perceived. Something must cue our expectations. An explanation, in other words, does not simply project the future on a screen in the present. We take the explanation with us into the future, and act on it if an occasion arises when it seems applicable. No magic is involved. Since it would be pointless to expect event A when the event is perceived, we must for some reason expect event *A* when we perceive some other event or set of events.

The referent that cues expectations about what is to come must be open to observation; nonperceivable cues would not be particularly useful. Linking an event to an abstract structure like an Oedipus complex cannot provide an explanation for the event; there is no perception that would trigger expectations unless the meaning of "Oedipus complex" is defined fully in empirical terms—in which case it could be dropped as otiose. When an explanation is used to create understanding of the past, the presence of an event in an empirical situation containing the connections included in the explanation accounts for the event. Given a good explanation, perception of specified cues in the future will lead us to expect particular events; perception of the same cues, and the event, in a description of the past, leads us to "understand" why the event occurred. Pragmatic success is the prime criterion for judging the adequacy and reliability of the explanation.

Although an explanation must relate observables to observables, it cannot consist of a concatenation of classifications and relational propositions taken from an empirical description. The relational propositions that appear in descriptions are limited in time, and specific in form—they relate *particular* values of the variables. The relational statements used in an explanation must be general or timeless if they are to be used in the future as well as the past. Explanations will always refer to descriptions, but their parts are logically distinct from the elements in a description.

The minimal requirements for adequate explanation, then, are: (1) an empirical description containing both classifications and relational propositions linking two or more of the events in the description, and a record of change; (2) an explanatory mechanism that can generate expectations that have empirical relevance.

Systems

The instrument that makes explanation possible is here called a *system*. It is defined as a formal logical structure, an abstract calculus that is totally unrelated to anything in the empirical world. The system, as a system, says nothing whatever about empirical events; it generates expectations within its own boundaries. Since the instrument used for explanation of empirical events must contain timeless or general propositions, and since it must generate expectations that can be warranted or justified, there is really no choice of instruments involved. Of all the structures that man can create, only a formal calculus can create warranted expectations. Given the axioms of a formal logical structure, certain conclusions are inescapable; if the axioms are accepted, the conclusions can be denied only by self-contradiction. *Within the calculus,* and only within the calculus, expectations about the effect of interacting variables can be justified completely. Barring errors in calculation, the entailments of a logical system are necessarily and indefeasibly true.

The key to the explanatory process, when the system paradigm is employed, is the generation of expectations within a formal calculus and the transfer of those expectations, under suitable conditions, to the empirical world. The transposition must, of course, be justified, and in the last analysis that justification is pragmatic. The best argument for using an explanation is that it works, it enables us to achieve our goals or purposes, though there are complex considerations involved that will be examined more fully below.

Both the system paradigm and the deductive paradigm depend on an effective merger of the power of logic to generate expectations or inferences and the hard facts of observation. In the deductive paradigm, fusion takes place at the level of the generalization; a generalization stipulates the logic of a relationship between two events. In the system paradigm, logic and observation merge at the level of a system—a network of interactions in which the two-element generalization is merely a special case. Three major points of difference appear between the two paradigms. First, the system paradigm does not depend on induction, on the generation of general statements from particular facts. Second, and more important, the focus of inquiry is changed radically. The deductive paradigm focuses attention on the common features of classes of events and tends to lead to the examination of a representative sample of the members of a class. The system paradigm is focused on the web of relations surrounding a single event, and examination of other members of the class does nothing to increase the power of the explanation—it serves mainly to eliminate random variations from the description of the empirical situation. Finally, the deductive paradigm construes the explanatory process in hierarchical terms, beginning with dyadic generalizations at the bottom while the system paradigm is expressed in terms of complex networks. A theorist using the deductive paradigm must attempt to create slots or chutes into which particular data can be fitted. A theorist using the system paradigm seeks to create a network that can be matched against the empirical situation in which the event to be explained appears. These distinctions may seem minor, but the deductive paradigm is much more demanding or constraining, since explanation cannot begin until suitable generalizations are available. And most important of all, partial or incomplete system explanations may still be quite useful, while a partial deductive explanation is wholly useless. It is this latter characteristic of system explanations that makes them particularly valuable in social science.

Systems and conceptual frameworks. A system consists of a set of variables $(V_1, V_2, V_3 \ldots V_n)$ and a set of rules that define the interactions among those variables $(R_1, R_2, R_3 \ldots R_n)$. Notation is shown in Figure 1. The round

$$\begin{pmatrix} V_1 V_2 V_3 \ldots V_n \\ R_1 R_2 R_3 \ldots R_n \end{pmatrix} \supset \phi$$

FIGURE 1

brackets enclosing the set ( ) indicate that the system is formal and *closed*. In a closed system, any change in the value of one of the variables in the set can be accounted for *completely* in terms of changes in the values of the other variables. The entailment of the system $(\supset \phi)$ can be any outcome of the interaction of the variables. An explanatory system does not entail one event and not others; manipulation of the elements of the system produces a number of entailments and every entailment is equally valid within the system. When a system is applied to an empirical situation it is not enough to show that one particular entailment of the system can be found in the empirical situation—that would mean that the system was a forecasting device and not an explanation. The aim is to match the total explanatory system with an empirical situation so that all of the entailments of the system have empirical counterparts in observation. The goal in explanation is a perfect match or fit between a complete system and a description rather than a logical fit between a single event and a general proposition, as in the deductive paradigm.

Systems are formal logical structures, like geometry or arithmetic or any other mathematical system. All systems are by definition closed and finite; otherwise there could be no entailment. In principle, systems are fully calculable, though in practice large systems may be calculable only in part—chess, for example, is a closed logical structure that cannot be fully calculated. No system contains unknown variables and none of the rules of interaction is unspecified. The variables in a system are formal symbols that have no empirical meaning; their meaning is defined solely within the framework of the calculus. When systems are used in explanation, these symbols must be given empirical meaning. That is, the terms of the calculus must be loaded with concepts that have empirical relevance. At this point, the formal calculus and an empirical description are brought together. Since this is one of the more delicate and critical aspects of explanation, full discussion of the problems of loading are reserved for the following chapter.

Although systems are always closed sets, it is useful for some purposes to think of open sets of closed systems —what are here called conceptual frameworks and indicated by the use of square brackets [ ]. The conceptual framework is "open" in the sense that it is incomplete, that new systems may always be added to the complex. Each system in an open set will be closed and will provide an explanation for a given class of events. The total conceptual framework defines the explanatory and conceptual apparatus that the individual uses to deal with his observations or ruminations. In addition to closed systems, conceptual frameworks will include incomplete systems, or imperfect systems; in fact, there are usually far more imperfect than closed systems in any individual's total conceptual apparatus.

"Conceptual framework" is a very useful concept. It is often possible to specify quite accurately the conceptual framework that a given individual uses to deal with given classes of phenomena, whether the individual is an optical physicist or a working politician. The structure of inquiry can usually be specified in terms of the development of appropriate or adequate systems within a conceptual framework, and examination of the actual content of a conceptual framework can often have quite useful results. In the treatment of psychotic patients, for example, one of the prime tasks of the psychiatrist is to learn how the patient "views the world," or "defines the situation." Comparison of the patient's "world view" with that of presumably "normal" persons can give the psychiatrist useful insights into the kinds of conceptual distortions that occur within the patient's mind. Similarly, explanations of human behavior can usually be formulated in terms of the conceptual framework which the individual uses to define the situation in which he finds himself and to react to it. Identification and classification of the major conceptual frameworks employed in a given society or culture is one of the major tasks in most of the social sciences—though the task is not always construed in these terms. Every person must have some explanatory base, however faulty, for his behavior; we all perform calculations of one sort or another when our behavior rises above the level of conditioned responses. By making explicit the form and content of these calculations, we might go a very long way toward adequate explanation of wide ranges of human behavior.

Using the concept system

As the term "system" is defined in the system paradigm of explanation, formal systems perform the functions that are usually attributed to "theories" in the deductive paradigm. The nomenclature is less significant than the performance, certainly, and it is pointless to ask what a theory "really" is, but well-established systems should probably be called "theories" if the concept is to be used at all. Because of the ambiguity of common usage, the term "theory" is used sparingly in the remainder of the essay, though I would myself define a theory as an instrument able to produce useful explanations.

Similarly, the term "system" is widely used in the social sciences and in a variety of ways. It is therefore necessary to indicate in greater detail the characteristics and limitations of "systems" as they are defined here. A system is not defined by its capacity to predict or explain but by its internal logical structure; no system is necessarily useful in explanation though all explanations make use of systems. Any set of two or more variables and one or more rules of interaction is a system. Given two variables (A and B) and one rule of interaction (A is the inverse of B), the system is complete and there are two entailments: if the value of A does not change, the value of B will not change; if the value of A is stipulated, the value of B is the inverse of the value of A. Whether any use could be found for this particular system I cannot say. In all probability, systems are usually constructed with particular events in mind and not created without purpose (except by mathematicians). But that has nothing to do with their identification as systems.

As system is defined here, it is incompatible with the conception of a system as a "black box" into which "inputs" flow and from which "outputs" may emanate, with or without "feedback." A system is a complete, self-contained set of variables; nothing moves into or out of the system and the notion of an "external" influence is a contradiction in terms since the system would then be open. The "black box" concept of system, which is very popular, implies an entity on which forces act, and which moves by reaction to those forces—the analogy is to Newtonian mechanics. This concept of system carries with it the danger that systems will be construed as empirical entities, and no set of empirical entities can be wholly isolated from the environment. Further, it requires the use of fairly complex notions like "feedback" to handle certain kinds of interactions and a small increase in the number of "feedback circuits" (four or five at most) renders the system incalculable. The concepts used in the "black box" definition of system are easily handled within our system paradigm. An "input" is simply a change in the value of one of the system variables; an "output" is a change of exactly the same sort. "Feedback" appears as a set of rules governing changes in the values of the variables in which time-order is stipulated. The notion of "system interaction," which is a logical impossibility in terms of our definition, can be handled by constructing larger systems in which independent entities appear as subsystems. The advantage in the system paradigm is that the larger system provides a framework in which the meaning of system interactions can be specified; lacking some wider context, system interactions are impossible to manage unless the systems are conceptually identical. Until it can be established that two entities are members of some common class, no comparison can be made of them; comparisons of any two things can only be made in terms of the defining properties of the classes in which they share membership. If both things have dimensionality, for example, they can be compared with respect to size.

Every system is based upon a set of fundamental variables (or terms) and a set of rules. The basic terms define the boundaries of the system, though the choice is not relevant to empirical considerations unless the system is intended for explanation. No proposition is part of the system unless it contains one of the basic terms; all propositions entailed by the interaction of the variables are part of the system. There is no "boundary problem." When systems are applied, the question of whether or not the elements in the empirical description are sufficiently detached from the environment to be amenable to explanation is very important, but that can only be determined by observation and that is not what is usually meant by a "boundary problem."

Finally, and it cannot be too strongly emphasized, there are no empirical or natural systems. No set of empirical propositions constitutes a system. In the empirical world, no set of classifications or variables can be isolated completely from the surrounding environment; it is never possible to stipulate *all* of the influences that may act on a particular variable. Everything, in a way, is related to everything else. No set of empirical propositions can have any formal entailment; entailments occur within the logical sector of explanation, not in the empirical sector. Happily, the relations among variables in the empirical world are not all of the same strength. Some sets of variables can be isolated from the remainder fairly well and that is what makes explanation a practical possibility. But the isolation is always imperfect, the set of variables is always incomplete. It follows that the fit between a logical structure and an empirical situation is always imperfect. Explanations, therefore, are always problematic. That is the reason why criteria are needed for evaluating the degree of fit between system and description. In terms of the system paradigm, explanation is possible if we assume that a formal system is isomorphic to an empirical situation. That assumption is known to be false, but the level of isomorphism at which it is true can be less than perfect without destroying the usefulness of the system. By referring to the purpose of inquiry, by insisting that explanations make control over events possible in principle, criteria can be provided which justify the assumption of isomorphism. The more fully the purpose is specified, and the more accurately the explanation permits events to be controlled, the stronger the justification for assuming that a system is an isomorph for an empirical situation.

SYSTEM EXPLANATION: AN ILLUSTRATION

The system paradigm of explanation requires the fusion of two elements, one logical and one empirical, in a three-step process. First, the phenomenon to be explained must be embedded in an empirical description that is dynamic and not static, that stipulates changes as well as differences. The phenomenon will be defined in terms of such changes. Second, a system, a formal calculus, is used to generate entailments or expectations with reference to a set of symbols. Third, the symbols or variables in the calculus are "loaded," given empirical referents, so that the entailments of the formal system have empirical meaning defined in terms of the concepts used to load the basic symbols. If the loaded system is isomorphic to the situation in which the phenomenon occurs, the system provides an explanation for the event. Assuming that the description is accurate, and that the formal system is logically consistent, explanation is achieved by showing that:

1. If the terms of an abstract calculus are loaded with a given set of concepts, each linked by rules of correspondence to specific empirical perceptions, the rules of interaction of the variables in the system are matched by the relational propositions in the description.
2. Within the loaded system, the phenomenon to be explained appears as a formal entailment.
3. Other entailments of the loaded system are matched by observations within the empirical situation.

The perfect isomorphism between loaded system and empirical situation implied in this account of the process is never attained in practice. The question that concerns us at this point, however, is whether an explanation (as defined above) is really achieved when these conditions have been satisfied.

Clearly, the loaded system produces expectations that are relevant to the empirical world through the meaning of the concepts used to load the system. The expectations are justified because the system demonstrates that given variables, interacting according to stipulated rules, will lead formally to a particular outcome. The empirical meaning of the variables also makes possible intervention and control in principle over the situation by indicating which elements in the empirical situation could be modified to produce different results. The explanation, in brief, makes explicit the implicit logic of the empirical situation, *as it has been conceptualized.* If the description is accurate, and the rules of interaction are as stated, then no other outcome could be expected than the event that actually did occur. If a different outcome did emerge, some error has been committed. Either the concepts are inaccurate, the rules of interaction have not been correctly defined (in the empirical situation), or the phenomenon is inadequately described.

An illustration will help clarify the process and perhaps indicate the enormous power of what may appear as a fairly simple or even trite procedure. The example is taken from physical science. It seemed wise to avoid argument about the adequacy of the explanation used as an example, and there are few cases in social science where a given explanation is almost universally accepted. Moreover, the example underlines nicely the extent to which the system paradigm fits the pattern of explanation that physical science has developed. The reader need not be familiar with the illustration, though it usually appears in even the most rudimentary course in physical science at the secondary school level.

The phenomenon to be explained is a change in the amount of illumination provided by a light bulb. The description of the empirical situation contains two changes: one is the increase in illumination, the other an increase in the number of batteries in the circuit containing the bulb. Note that there must be *two* changes; if only one change was included in the description, nothing could be

used to cue our expectations about the event—the change
in illumination would be due to something outside the
description. The question is, can the phenomenon be explained? Is an increase in illumination to be expected
under the circumstances? In a very simple case of this
kind, the inadequacy of the deductive paradigm is apparent. To suggest a search for an empirical generalization
covering the class of events "increase in illumination from
light bulbs" could be extremely misleading. And even if it
were established that "illumination from light bulbs always increases when more batteries are added to the
circuit," an inquirer would still be entitled to ask for
reasons why the change occurs. He would then be re-
ferred to electromagnetic theory. And at that point the
deductive explanation would closely parallel a system explanation—as I hope to show. My point here is that the
focus on a search for "empirical generalizations" is poor
strategy in inquiry since it points the observer in the
direction of examining an n of instances rather than concentrating his attention on the essentials of a particular
situation.

The illustration makes use of a well-established system
or theory. How the system came to be established in the
first place will be examined in the following two chapters.
For the moment, we can concentrate on the way in which
explanations are made when accepted systems or theories
are at hand.

The empirical situation, including the phenomenon to
be explained, can be structured symbolically to facilitate
precise discussion; concepts like "number," "amount,"
"battery," etc. are used in their everyday meaning. The
relevant variables in the situation (we know they are
relevant through the system or theory that is used to

explain the event) are light bulbs, batteries, and illumination. One relational proposition is needed to link the increase in the number of batteries in the circuit and the increase in the amount of illumination emanating from the bulb. The "link" is only a descriptive conjunction of perceptions. If no established system were available, an endless variety of other factors might be included in the description—the number of observers, time of day, geographic location, etc. Because we have an explanation for the phenomenon, they are known not to be related to the amount of light provided by the bulb, or at least we know that their influence is so slight that it can be ignored. Under some circumstances, exclusion of elements in the empirical situation can be very tricky, even in physical science, since influences usually considered slight become significant as the level of precision of measurement increases. When no explanation is available, trial and error, augmented by associations inferred from analogous situations, serves as an editing mechanism in the first instance.

In skeletal form, the description is quite simple:

V_1 = The number of batteries in the circuit.
V_2 = Amount of illumination provided by the bulb.
R_1 = An increase in the value of V_1 was followed by an increase in the value of V_2.

The description could be made much more accurate by using a variety of instruments and providing numerical figures for each value of each variable and for the amount of increase in illumination to be expected for any change in value of V_1. The phenomenon to be explained is the change in the value of V_2. The request for an explanation takes the form: "Given the empirical situation, is a change in the value of V_2 to be expected when the value of V_1

changes?" The question is answered, using the system paradigm, by showing that if the empirical situation is assumed to correspond to a particular formal system, and that system is loaded accordingly with empirically relevant concepts, the change would be expected. The justification for making the assumption is complex, and in the last analysis, pragmatic.

The abstract calculus used to explain the phenomenon consists of five variables and three rules of interaction. Actually, the system used in physics is somewhat more complex but the simplification will serve our purposes well enough and avoid complicating the example. The calculus takes the following form:

GIVEN: V_1 V_2 V_3 V_4 V_5
     R_1: V_1 is the product of V_2 and V_3
     R_2: V_4 varies directly as V_1
     R_3: V_5 varies directly as V_4
THEREFORE: An increase in V_5 is to be expected if V_1 increases.

Since the system is already established, the other entailments can be ignored. Note that each of the variables appears in one of the rules of the system; it would be pointless to include a variable without a rule. Similarly, each rule includes at least one of the basic terms of the system and no terms that are not part of the set. The system must be closed if we are to produce logical inferences. The system is wholly formal; none of the elements or basic terms has any empirical meaning at this point. Given the system, the canons of formal logic warrant the assertion that an increase in the value of V_5 is to be expected when the value of V_1 increases.

The formal system must now be combined with the

empirical description so that expectations can be transferred from the calculus to the empirical world. The procedure involves the same problems, and the same limitations, as the application of any mathematical system to empirical data. It *does not* involve the induction problem. The explanatory process is simply a form of applied logic or mathematics, when the system paradigm is used. Explanation is a form of calculation. That is what gives explanation its power, and supplies theorists with a justification for the assumptions required in explanation.

The coupling between logic and empirical description is supplied by loading the basic terms in the calculus with empirical concepts—giving meaning to the variables. The rules of the calculus need not be loaded, obviously, though they must parallel or encompass the relational propositions included in the description. The concepts used to load the calculus need not be precisely the same as those used in the description; they may be "wider" or more general. Each concept must be linked to the empirical world by a set of rules of correspondence that specify the perceptions that identify the concept. The formal skeleton remains unchanged, and all of the entailments generated by the calculus are formal and not empirical. In effect, the calculus is loaded on the assumption that the empirical situation in which the phenomenon appears can be paralleled within the calculus, that identification of the basic terms of the calculus with specified empirical variables will produce results that have empirical relevance and usefulness. Once the terms are loaded with concepts, if the rules of interaction are parallel to the relational propositions in the description, the expectations generated by the calculus have an empirical counterpart. If the phenomenon appears among those expectations, we have an explanation.

A system explanation can be viewed as a formal pattern, a map, that can be imposed or overlaid on the empirical world. If the pattern fits the empirical data, it serves as an explanation or guide to the empirical events that fall within the pattern. At any time, present, past, or future, that the pattern of empirical events recurs, the same pattern will provide an explanation for them. When enough of the empirical situation is identified to justify the belief that it falls under a particular pattern, the unobserved implications of that pattern are to be expected—that is where system explanations derive their predictive power. Note that there is no need to become involved in either the problem of induction or the search for empirical generalizations. Nor does the explanation refer to a sequence of events. What is explained is a particular event. The explanation will then hold for every event that falls into the same class. The class in turn is defined by the terms of the explanation, not by any criteria external to the explanation.

To explain an increase in illumination when batteries are added to an electric circuit, the formal calculus is loaded in the following way:

LET: V_1 = Amount of voltage in the circuit.
V_2 = Amount of current in the circuit.
V_3 = Amount of resistance in the circuit.
V_4 = Temperature of bulb filament.
V_5 = Amount of illumination provided by bulb.

Each concept (voltage, current, etc.) must be linked to specific empirical indicators by rules of correspondence that will be omitted here. The rules of interaction remain the same, though they acquire meaning because the basic terms in the system have been given meanings:

R_1: Voltage = Current × resistance.

R_2: An increase in voltage will increase the temperature of the bulb filament.

R_3: An increase in filament temperature will lead to an increase in illumination.

THEREFORE: An increase in voltage will be followed by an increase in illumination.

Ignoring limits, if we assume that the system is isomorphic to the empirical situation, a change in the amount of illumination is to be expected if a change in the amount of voltage occurs. The event is explained. Conversely, since a change in voltage was followed by a change in illumination, that provides evidence for the isomorphism of system and empirical situation. Circularity is broken by referring to other factors outside the particular empirical situation, e.g., to other similar empirical situations, to relevant and related explanations of other events, to various tests or experiments in which the implications for controlling the situation contained in the explanation can be extended and tested.

Note that the concepts used to load the system differ from the concepts used in the description—voltage instead of batteries, for example. That is a normal condition, perhaps because the concepts used in descriptions are likely to be taken from common usage, particularly in social science, and may not be particularly useful for explanation, that is, may define classes of events in terms that cannot readily be used to formulate explanations. Rules are needed, obviously, to link the two sets of concepts. In effect, the rules of correspondence that link the concepts used to load the system must be identical to or wider than the rules that link the concepts used in description to empirical observations. Since it was stipulated at the outset that the explanation was well established, questions about the validity of the explanation can be delayed. The purpose of the example was to indicate the kinds of relations and activities involved in the explanatory process.

The three elements in an explanation, using an established system, are brought together in Figure 2. Note that

Empirical situation	Loaded system	Formal calculus
V_1 = no. of batteries	V_1 = amt. of voltage	GIVEN: V_1, V_2, V_3,
V_2 = amt. of	V_2 = amt. of current	V_4, V_5
illumination	V_3 = amt. of	R_1: $V_1 = V_2$ times V_3
R_1 = V_1 varied	resistance	R_2: V_4 varies directly
directly as V_2	V_4 = filament temp.	with V_1
ϕ = An increase in	V_5 = amt.	R_3: V_5 varies directly
V_1 led to an	illumination	with V_4
increase in V_2	R_1: $V_1 = V_2$ times	THEREFORE: V_5 varies
	V_3	directly as V_1
	R_2: V_4 varies	
	directly as V_1	
	R_3: V_5 varies	
	directly as V_4	
	ϕ: An increase in V_1	
	leads to an	
	increase in V_5	
	Plus: Rules of correspondence linking each concept used in the loading to particular observations.	

FIGURE 2

the rules of interaction function in exactly the same way however the calculus is loaded. The calculus, in other words, does not produce *empirical* inferences. Logically, the same result would be obtained if "roses" were substituted for the term "voltage" wherever it occurs. The results would be nonsense, empirically, but the logic of the structure would remain consistent. The validity of an application of a calculus depends on the loading, and errors in loading affect the usefulness of the result, not the logic of the system. Of course, if the calculus is loaded "properly" and the results still do not fit the empirical situation, then the wrong calculus may have been chosen, and alterations will have to be made in it before it can serve as an explanation for that particular situation.

All of the other implications of the loaded system can also be paralleled in the empirical world—that is implied by the term "established system." If voltage, resistance, and current are measured carefully, the rule of interaction ($E = IR$) will hold. This suggests one of the important uses of explanations: their implications are in fact predictions about the content of an empirical situation, therefore they tell us where to look and what to expect. Predictions can be tested against findings. They serve also to call attention to relations or consequences that may have been overlooked in the descriptive process. The interplay of theoretical and empirical considerations involved here is typical of many aspects of the explanatory process. Fitting a system to an empirical situation necessarily requires us to move back and forth from one to the other. In the process, the quality of the explanation, and our knowledge of the empirical situation, may be improved.

The system used as an example fully satisfies all of the criteria of explanation set forth in the previous chapter. And every scientific explanation meets the same requirements, so far as I have been able to determine. The phenomenon to be explained is a logical consequence of the interaction of known variables according to stipulated rules, and any phenomenon that appears in an empirical environment isomorphic to the loaded system is explained by it. And the loaded system suggests a variety of ways in which the amount of illumination might be controlled. It can be increased (to a point) by adding more batteries, or by decreasing the amount of resistance in the circuit. It can be decreased by eliminating batteries, by increasing the amount of resistance, or by changing the material in the bulb filament. The system is open to experimental check since the empirical elements can be isolated and changes predicted by the system can be put to the pragmatic test. Experimentation also provides a way to increase the precision of the explanation. If careful measurements can be made of each value of the variables, the precision of the rules of interaction can also be increased, with a corollary increase in the precision of the whole explanation.

The explanation, as we might expect, borders on the edge of circularity; reference to concrete or empirical observations provides a base point and saves the system. Explanations are tautologies, philosophically speaking, and we are seeking to define the conditions under which a tautology can be put to good use. We use them by moving back and forth between the tautology and the empirical world, trying to create an isomorph for the empirical situation. One serves to check on the other, and in the last analysis the results of observation must be honored. At the beginning of the explanatory process, the justification for assuming isomorphism between system and empirical situation is likely to be thin. As the web of relations is spun out through testing, experimentation, reference to history, or application to other examples, the system is modified by the results of using the system and the justification for assuming isomorphism acquires strength. In a well-established discipline like physics, the web is so thick that its tautological base is hardly apparent—until we begin prying into fundamentals. As the theoretical structure available in a field grows more complex, judgments about the adequacy of fit between system and observation are more readily made since there are more reference points to check against. But in the last analysis, the justification lies in the use that can be made of the system, the purposes that the explanation will serve.

Explanations that make use of established systems demonstrate the basic structure of the explanatory process. But we need to look more closely at the way an explanation unfolds when no established system is available, and at the criteria that are applied to different parts of the process. We must, in other words, concern ourselves with ways of making qualitative distinctions among explanations. In a deductive explanation, all that must be done is to establish the fact that a given structure meets the criteria of explanation, for there are no qualitative distinctions among them. Using the system paradigm, the quality of explanations varies greatly and we must take the purpose of inquiry into consideration before that quality can be judged. The extent to which the explanation provides control over the environment, the limitations on its application, depends in part on particular circumstances, but some of the more general criteria of adequacy that an explanation must satisfy can be specified in advance, as we shall see in the next two chapters.

CHAPTER FOUR

THE PROCESS OF EXPLANATION

CONSIDERED as a process rather than a structure, explanation is a very complex form of activity for which no rules can be specified that will guarantee success. Explanation is a creative and not a mechanical or logical process. To use an analogy, explanations are intellectual tools and the creation of explanations resembles toolmaking. Like any other tool, an explanation is created for a purpose—unless like Rube Goldberg's creations, it is intended only to amuse. Tool design depends on the purpose for which the tool is intended and the situation in which it will be used. Nevertheless, there are certain principles that toolmakers follow, certain criteria that can be applied to all toolmaking. Similarly, we can stipulate some of the general criteria of explanation even though the requirements of a specific explanation are not known.

This chapter is concerned with these basic principles of explanation. The discussion is intended in part to provide guidelines for theory construction, and in part to indicate the points in an explanation where criticism needs to be directed. The organization of the discussion implies no necessary order for the explanatory process;

no one can say in advance how an explanation should be built. Once the explanation is completed, it is open to both logical and empirical criticism. We want to know first whether the structure meets the criteria of explanation, whether it actually provides an explanation for an event. Beyond that, we need to know whether the explanation will hold, whether it is a "good" explanation, and within what limits.

The basic elements of the explanatory process can be identified readily enough but they are empirically inseparable. Each element is contingent on all of the others. Analytically, however, there must first be an event that requires explanation, and certain descriptive requirements must be fulfilled before explanation is possible. The point may seem trivial, but the maxim "no phenomenon, no explanation" is often violated in social science—particularly by those who search for "general" explanations. Second, a logical system is needed that is internally consistent and able to generate entailments. Third, the calculus must be loaded with concepts that have empirical relevance. Finally, the loaded system must be fitted to the empirical situation, and its uses and limits established.

THE EVENT TO BE EXPLAINED

A request for an explanation can take a variety of forms, though the instrument that can satisfy the request will appear as a system. When an event has already occurred in the past, the question is usually, "How or why did that change occur?" But if the question is phrased in the form, "How can that situation be changed?" it requires the same explanation. The form in which the question appears has a great deal to do with our capacity to answer it—to formulate an explanation. For example, I may be able to answer the question, "How can the distribution of income in society be changed?" because it does not specify the kind of change that is desired, but unable to supply an explanation that would answer the question, "How can the distribution of income in society be changed so that poverty (suitably defined) is eliminated without reducing the level or quality of capital investment?" The more precisely a question is framed, the more precise the explanation needed to answer it. And the terms of the question, obviously, depend on the purpose of the questioner.

Explanations always and necessarily begin with a concrete event, a change, some alteration in the environment that commands attention. It may be, of course, that a system is already available to explain the event, but inquiry does not consist of scouring the empirical world, loaded system in hand, looking for events to explain—as though systematic study were equivalent to a turkey shoot. In fact, once an explanation is well established, the events that it can explain are no longer very interesting from the theorist's point of view, and no one familiar with the explanation will find the events it explains in any way extraordinary and worth attention. What attracts attention is the unexplained event, the event that appears to contradict existing explanations, the events whose consequences we wish to control.

While the number of events in the environment that might serve as objects of inquiry is in principle limitless, not every event is worth explaining, nor is every event necessarily explicable. Focusing inquiry, as graduate students learn to their sorrow, is a difficult matter—particularly in those cases where the choice must be justified.

The grounds for selecting one event or another may be theoretical or utilitarian. "I find it interesting" is a puerile substitute for a justification and tradition is no justification at all. It is a valid criticism of an explanation, and of the person who offers it, that no one familiar with the field cares whether or not it is either acceptable or available. The criteria by which events are selected for inquiry are an important part of methodology.

The implications of the assumption that events selected for explanation should be significant are worth considering further. Significance may be a product of normative judgment or evaluation, or a consequence of the theoretical structures employed in a discipline. If explanations are defined as instruments that make possible control in principle over the environment, then the events that are worth explaining are those men wish to control. Social evaluation, which has as its object the identification of events in the environment that should be inhibited or facilitated by individuals and institutions in society, lies at the very heart of empirical inquiry. Explanation is the servant of evaluation and the two are never fully dissociated, though the desire for control should not interfere with criticism or the critical faculty. Even the physical sciences, in their early history, show the normative and utilitarian precepts in which they originated.

Once a substantial body of theory is available in a field, the choice of events to be explained may be controlled in part by the lacunae in the explanatory structure. Such theoretical considerations are of considerable importance in some of the physical sciences. But in the undeveloped fields, and perhaps most particularly in social science, concentration on events whose control is urgently required on utilitarian or normative grounds is both understandable and justifiable. Indeed, it is hard to see what arguments might be adduced in favor of a different strategy of inquiry. We seek control over those events that for some reason we wish to control; those reasons will almost certainly be normative.

The suggestion that social science should seek deliberately to gain control over events on the basis of normative judgments will doubtless conjure once again the specter of social engineering and totalitarian control over the life of the individual, particularly for the doctrinaire liberal. It is time to say most emphatically that in this context the liberal tradition is antiquated and inadequate, if indeed it ever was a viable doctrine. There is a world of difference between a social science that is a creature of government, in the sense that Lysenko and his cohorts provided intellectual support and justification for the dogmas of the Soviet government at the expense of intellectual integrity and honesty, and a social science that provides the knowledge that is required to eliminate undesirable social consequences and facilitate desirable social effects. Granted the difficulty of deciding what is desirable and what is not, much of the difficulty can be laid at the doorstep of an inadequate social science—a social science, be it said, that sometimes appears almost psychotically fearful of becoming useful.

The chief argument against a deliberate attempt to control the social environment is the danger of abuse; in this respect the situation is parallel to the reaction against the development of atomic energy. The argument will not stand criticism. Every tool can be abused, whether it is the surgeon's knife or the psychologist's explanation of human behavior. Any increase in human knowledge, in man's ability to control the environment, carries some risk. But it also carries potential benefits, and even if it did not, there could be no good argument for a deliberate restriction of inquiry because there is no way to tell in advance what inquiry is likely to produce, or how the results of inquiry might be used.

Singular events and classes

Do we explain a single event? Or a class? An explanation does both, but only in the sense that it provides an explanation for a class of events by virtue of its capacity to explain every event in the class. The difficulty arises with the concept "class." If an event is explained adequately, it will explain every other identical event; a map that is accurate for a given area continues to be accurate unless the area changes. The class of events that an explanation can handle is defined by the terms of the explanation. Classes that have been defined for other purposes, or inherited from tradition, may not be explicable as classes. In such cases, it may be quite useful to subdivide the class, or break it up, and redefine classes that are open to explanation.

Formally, the difficulty lies in the fact that a class is defined by a set of characteristics or properties; any object that has those properties (among others) is a member of the class. The defining properties of the class provide the only properties in which an explanation could be framed that would be applied to the whole class. If a class consists of objects with properties A, B, and C, for example, an explanation that will hold for the class must also be formulated in terms of A, B, and C. That is the great difficulty with explanations of voting behavior. The class "vote" is defined by a physical action that has a certain significance within a given associational context. An explanation for *all* votes would have to be formulated in terms of those physical actions. If voting is broken down, however, it becomes much more amenable to explanation, and that, of course, is what is done in practice. That is the principal reason for suggesting that it is probably good strategy to begin with the single event rather than with a class of events, unless the class has been defined with a particular explanation in mind.

When the deductive paradigm is employed, class explanations can be very troublesome, particularly in those areas where classes are complex and heterogeneous. To explain voting behavior using the deductive paradigm, for example, generalizations are needed that will hold for all members of the class. Given the way in which "vote" is defined, that is extremely difficult. In effect, a generalization that holds for the whole class would be an additional defining property of the class; since it is obvious that the class "vote" contains human acts of grossly different character, once the definition of the term goes beyond the simple act of casting a vote, such generalizations are unlikely. "Probabilistic" generalizations, which apply to part of the class, can be used to deal with aggregate behavior, though weakly because the deductions that can be made from them are limited. They are useless for explaining the behavior of individual voters. The system paradigm attacks the problem from a different direction, searching for classes of votes that are homogeneous with respect to a particular explanation—family influence, for example. By dividing the class "votes," explanations can be produced for subclasses and then combined.

The system paradigm is equally advantageous when events are described in statistical or probabilistic terms. In the deductive paradigm, where empirical generalizations are considered *part of* the logical apparatus, probabilistic descriptions create formidable logical hurdles since deductive inference is severely limited. In the system paradigm, probabilistic statements are not needed *within* the logical structure. Invariant rules, applied to changing conditions, produce outcomes that are not invariant. The internal structure can remain formal and complete. And we may note that the scientist deals with the problem of statistical description in precisely the same way. The behavior of gases, for example, is described statistically. But the explanation offered for the behavior of gases is an idealized, formal structure in which relations are absolute —it is a mathematical system. The "probable" aspect of the explanation refers to the consequences of application, not to the internal structure of the explanation. The reliability of a system explanation will always appear as a fraction, since the homogeneity of empirical events cannot be guaranteed, but that causes no special problems for either theorist or user.

One of the more useful consequences of approaching explanation in this way is the elimination of the "argument from uniqueness," the claim that historians and social scientists deal with unique, nonrecurring events that cannot be explained by scientific methods. In part, the argument is merely misplaced, for explanations can deal with classes only by dealing with individual members of the class, even if they are directed at aggregates. And in any case, a valid explanation can be provided for a nonrecurring event when system explanation is used—and in some cases with deductive explanations as well. Neither the significance of an event, nor its availability for explanation, depends on the frequency with which it occurs. Further, increased frequency of occurrence does not permit a more powerful explanation. Multiple instances of an event are useful for canceling random variations in the empirical situation, and for testing an explanation, but there are various other factors in explanation that are equally important.

Describing the situation

Events to be explained must be embedded in a network of empirical relations, tied to events by relational statements. It is very important to be clear about the meaning of "embedding." The phenomenon will appear in the description as a change in the value of one or more variables, or a change in the composition of a set of variables. The explanation will consist of a set of variables; changes take place in the values of the variables according to the rules governing the operation of the set. The description of the empirical situation should therefore include all of the variables assumed to be related to the phenomenon, and a record of the changes that take place in their values over time. The relational statements need be no more than descriptions of constant conjunctions since the description cannot attribute causality to any given relationship. In effect, the explanatory system provides causal connections, since changes within the set can be attributed *logically* to the effect of particular variables.

How to decide what to include in or exclude from a description? If there is no theory available to provide guidelines, trial and error, experience, and knowledge of related events must be called upon. Analogies can be drawn to other situations in which relations are known; corollary theories may be examined for parallels. Any knowledge that is available can be used. Usually, there is no need to proceed without any guidance; there are always *some* grounds for choosing some variables rather than others. Once a start is made, inquiry can proceed by trial and error, hunch, insight, intuition, and any other procedure that human ingenuity can produce.

Once a tentative selection of variables is made, inquiry moves to the logical realm to see if a system can be constructed that will account for the set of changes included in the description. The results of logical manipulation may lead to changes in the descriptive set; some variables are added and others are dropped. Explanation is not a rigorous procedure and the inquirer may order his steps as he pleases. He can formulate a tentative explanation, test it in a preliminary way, then drop it, or try to elaborate it further. No one can say how the work is actually done.

A brief example will illustrate the range of possibilities. Consider the mother whose only son has lost his appetite. How to account for the change? The mother begins with descriptive information—a change in eating patterns. She has other information, but does not know what is relevant. As tentative explanations are formed, she appeals to various aspects of the available description of past events, seeking a pattern that will hold. Is the boy sick? More information is needed. A cool forehead, or a thermometer reading, leads to the rejection of that possibility. Is he in trouble? No: the school authorities or the police would by now have called, and in any case, the loss of appetite would in that case be sudden, but the loss of appetite was in fact gradual. She tries another tack entirely. Why do young boys lose their appetites? Sickness. Trouble. Love. Of course! He has a "crush" on some girl. *That's* why he's been combing his hair carefully before going to school; and she had noticed that his clothes looked neater. The case is explained, but not yet closed. That evening a gentle probe: "You're almost old enough to have a girl friend now . . . just think, my little boy . . . ." The response is gratifying—a startled look, a flush of color. The test establishes the explanation. Q.E.D.

A simple case of this kind brings out extremely well the interplay between theory and description. The mother has explanatory systems, a range of them; she has information about the past. She has a technique, a method of calculation, not formalized perhaps but intrinsically logical and orderly. The search is brief, the amount of information required fairly simple. But an attempt to explain how the distribution of ethnic and racial groups in American higher education could be changed would involve the same kinds of search procedures, the same interchange between possibilities and experience. It would probably take a sizable book to allow room for sorting out all of the factors involved in the study, and the resulting system would be a very complex affair, with a large number of subsystems, each comprising still more subsystems. But the basic structural unit would remain the same. The power of simple structures, suitably amplified, should not be underestimated; a computer is only a large collection of switches. Given principles of organization, simple structures become powerful levers for dealing with a complex environment.

CHOOSING A SYSTEM

The system used in an explanation, the logical calculus, may be borrowed from mathematics, adapted from another explanation, or created specifically for the inquiry in hand. The source of the system is irrelevant to the quality of the explanation; systems have no past to be weighed against present performance. Nor do we have to worry about the source of the general statements within the calculus since they do not have to be "empirical." Karl R. Popper makes a similar point with reference to the induction problem, for he argues that it is pointless to worry about the source of generalizations so long as they can be tested.[1] The position taken here is similar in principle but different in application, since the possibility of testing *empirical* generalizations is also denied. The inductionist's claim that timeless empirical generalizations are somehow extrapolated from specific facts by a potentially definable procedure is otiose within the context of the system paradigm. Doubtless, general propositions are somehow related to human experience; there is no other possible source for them. But Hume's argument seems beyond refutation, and the implication, surely, is that the search should be directed to locating or producing useful logical systems, not to determining how they are produced.

The adequacy of a system as an explanatory device cannot be decided on purely logical grounds; it depends also on empirical considerations. Logically, a system must be consistent and properly calculated. That is not always as easy as it may sound, particularly in extensive and complex systems—certain situations arise in mathematics, for example, in which it is impossible to say whether or not a given inference is compatible with the axioms of a calculus. So long as part of the system can be calculated,

---

[1]Karl R. Popper, *The Logic of Scientific Discovery* (Science Editions, 1961), Ch. 1.

however, it may be used in explanation; completeness is not essential.

The size and complexity of the logical system depend on the purpose at hand. In general, the rule of parsimony is probably a good guide, but excessive simplicity may force ambiguity since the concepts used to load the system are likely to be very broad when only a few variables are used. Further, simple systems may force the theorist to ignore known relations because there is no room in the system for them. The best way of handling the problem of complex systems, not surprisingly, is to break them into smaller elements that are amenable to calculation. Even where explanation begins from a very broad phenomenon (such as a major change in the distribution of resources within society) the resulting explanation is likely to be a complex set of sets and subsets. Whether it is better to begin from below, constituting simple explanations and combining them into complex wholes, or to break a complex whole into component parts, increasing the density of the network as the total system is subdivided, no one can say.

Social scientists rarely borrow systems directly from mathematics, though economists and even political scientists have in recent years shown some interest in the mathematical theory of games developed by von Neumann and Morgenstern, and in certain other branches of mathematics like Markov chains. In part, this may be a reflection of a prejudice against model building (a strategy disparaged by most noneconomists, but commended as excellent when the system paradigm of explanation is used); in part it can be ascribed to ignorance of mathematics among social scientists. But it must also be said that most of the available mathematical systems are not particularly useful for social science though they are applied extensively in physics. The mathematician, I am told, finds the problems that interest the social scientist either too simple and dull to work with or so complex and difficult as to be insoluble. New branches of mathematics might well develop if competent mathematicians developed an interest in social science—witness the impact of physics on the mathematics of the 20th century. For the present, the outlook is not promising, and most of what passes for mathematics in social science is no more than statistics in various guises. Only the economist seems to indulge in model or system building on any substantial scale.

For the immediate future, then, social scientists can probably expect to construct their own systems, with or without the assistance of the mathematicians. The problem sounds more formidable than is actually the case. The kinds of systems needed in the present state of the social sciences are likely to be fairly straightforward, not involving sophisticated or complex manipulations of the variables. The critical problem in explanation of any event is identification of the variables that are important in a given empirical situation and determining their rules of interaction. Knowledge of mathematics would doubtless be useful, since it would suggest interactions in a form that might not occur to the untrained social scientist. But the social scientist, not the mathematician, must specify the elements of the system and the rules of interaction since he is familiar with the field-relevant information and the mathematician is not. Systems are not constructed out of thin air, even in mathematics; inquiry begins with some notions, however vague and erroneous, about the structure of an empirical situation—if there were *nothing* to go on, it would be impossible even to begin. Systems may develop by successive increments or in sudden jumps; there is no rule. But they do get built. Much of the difficulty is conceptual rather than logical or mathematical. If suitable concepts can be found, systems can be created easily enough.

LOADING THE SYSTEM

The most important and most difficult part of explanation is the selection of concepts to load the system. The choice of systems, the content of the description, and the program of action for intervening in the empirical situation suggested by the explanation, are all contingent upon the concepts used in the explanation. Further, the range or scope of the explanation, its capacity to handle empirical events, depends absolutely on the concepts with which the system is loaded. Unfortunately, conceptualization is yet another aspect of the explanatory process in which no more than a few general guidelines can be offered as advice to the prospective theorist. The hazards are compounded for the social scientists by the fact that we customarily think about social affairs using concepts that are largely unexamined. That makes it possible to locate events worth explaining without first creating an explanation, but it also complicates the task of explanation at subsequent stages of inquiry.

Discussion of the problems of conceptualization has a long history in the social sciences, particularly in the form of argument about "approaches" to the study of given fields of specialization. That precommitment to a given set of concepts is desirable in social science seems dubious, though it might be possible to produce concepts with some general usefulness. Certainly the history of suggested general concepts—power, attitude, authority, etc.— is not very encouraging. It is also unlikely that a conceptual revolution will occur in social science, although there is a clear need for some new concepts in every field. In political science, for example, the split with economics left the economists in possession of most of the concepts related to the distribution and allocation of resources in society. Though the need for such concepts in the study of government may seem obvious, they have not been developed. Similar lacunae could doubtless be found in the other social sciences. Conceptual innovation is a serious need, however unlikely conceptual revolution may seem.

The general nature of the problem of conceptualization is readily stated. Somehow, the theorist must steer a course between the Scylla of excessive narrowness and the Charybdis of indefeasibility. If the concepts are too narrow, the explanation will not go very far beyond description; if the concepts are defined too broadly, the meaning of propositions that employ them tends to ambiguity and the explanation will not be defeasible. In description, narrowness and precision are an asset, other things equal; in explanation, however, that is not the case. If an explanatory system is loaded with the same concepts used to describe, a common practice in social science, the generality of the explanation will be low. A system using the concepts income, religious affiliation, party affiliation, parental party preference, and voting preference in the latest election will not be very useful except to explain voting behavior. A system loaded with such concepts as "the search for identity," alienation, anomie, helplessness, and rootlessness can be applied to almost any human action, but a price must be paid in precision. Unless these concepts can be linked firmly to some concrete indicators, they may not be defeasible and therefore may be worthless.

The principal tool for evaluating concepts is, of course, the requirement that an explanation using them provide control over the empirical situation to which the explanation is applied. It is easy to *account for* an event, to produce a conceptual structure in which the event is plausible; it is most difficult to produce concepts that provide a meaningful strategy of intervention that will permit control in principle over the situation. By adding this requirement to the defining terms of an explanation, we provide a workable criterion for sorting explanations according to their usefulness.

Some of the basic problems in conceptualization can best be demonstrated by a rather simple illustration. The aim is to show the importance of requiring control in principle over the event as a criterion of adequate explanation, and at the same time indicate the way in which the choice of concepts influences other aspects of the explanatory process, particularly the kind of intervention that should be taken to alter the situation.

Suppose that a serious "riot" erupts suddenly in a large American city. If a recurrence is to be prevented, as seems desirable, then the outburst must be explained. The concepts used in the explanation play an important part in deciding the best way to attack the problem. Consider the following possibilities:

1. First, conceptualize the situation as a riot, that is, use the same concept we have used to describe the situation. We must then search the empirical situation for other events that can be linked to riots. Posit that the city has

been visited frequently by agitators preaching racial violence as a means for achieving civil rights. A system is readily built in which extended agitation leads to violence. It is *an* explanation of the event, though its scope is very limited. It suggests that the way to prevent or inhibit riots is to inhibit agitation, particularly by outlanders. Police are very fond of this explanation; agitators are not, except perhaps when they are soliciting financial assistance. Will the explanation hold? It provides a strategy of intervention that would be difficult to test adequately unless agitation were very carefully defined, and in limited terms. Anyone who insisted on maintaining it would be hard to sway by argument, as would anyone who insisted that the explanation is worthless. The explanation is therefore not very useful, even if we ignore the fact that it contains but one factor and therefore forces the elimination of a variety of factors that are usually accepted as relevant to rioting.

2. If the "riot" is conceptualized as an example of violence, the scope of the explanation broadens enormously, as does the number of related variables—violence is a very common phenomenon. To explain the riot as an example of violence requires an explanation for all examples of violence. The explanation will apply to any war, riot, fistfight, or physical punishment of child by parent. For such general ills, broad causes are essential; we are forced to load the system with other concepts of equal generality or the result will be ludicrous. For lack of a better example, link violence to frustration; they are roughly of the same order. How to intervene? By eliminating frustration. What does that mean programmatically? That is a very difficult question to answer, even if the explanation is taken seriously and the system duly expanded. We have linked a concrete event (the riot) to an abstract concep-

tion (frustration) and not to another event. Until the meaning of frustration is spelled out in empirical terms, we do not have an explanation—only a heuristic device. The structure can account for the riot, but it cannot explain it.

So much said, it is also the case that broad conceptual structures of this kind, though they cannot explain, may still be very useful—more so, in fact, than simplistic structures such as (1). Explanation is not the only goal of inquiry. It would be most unfortunate if all heuristic and exploratory structures were eliminated from serious consideration merely because they do not explain. The term explanation should be reserved for structures that perform the functions of explanations, certainly, but the possibilities inherent in broad structures of this kind (to which I have not done justice here) deserve serious exploration in their own right. Careful study may produce typologies that can serve as the basis for subsystems that provide good explanations for certain kinds of behavior; indicators may be devised for measuring, however roughly, some of the elements in frustration and their effects. Perhaps nothing can be done in this particular case, but the class of cases should not be ignored. Such structures can help us decide what kinds of information are relevant to a given event, what kinds of relations need to be established before we can understand and control them. Complex social phenomena are unlikely to be amenable to simplistic explanations, however much we are prepared to honor Occam's razor.

Returning to our example, the consequences of narrowing or widening the scope of the concepts used in explanation can be demonstrated endlessly. If the "riot" is explained in terms of a chain reaction, failure to stifle initial, minor outbursts may be held accountable for the whole and an increase in the police force urged as a preventative strategy—ignoring the host of ancillary questions raised by the heuristic structure in (2). If the riots are taken as evidence of deepseated hopelessness and rage against the white community on the part of the Negro, the explanation may suggest that nothing can be accomplished in the short run and that society ought to turn its attention to the long-range causes of the outburst. Without some criterion such as capacity to intervene in the situation as a guide, it would be literally impossible to weigh one explanation against another.

FITTING THE SYSTEM

In practice, systems are designed to fit particular situations, or selected to approximate them. By the time we have a fully loaded system available, it should approximate the empirical situation fairly closely. The task of explanation is not completed, however, even if the fit between system and empirical situation is very tight—in those cases where the system has not yet been established. For one thing, the fit is never perfect and we need to account for differences between expectations and findings when the system is tested. Moreover, every situation can be explained in a number of different ways, and some hold better than others, for given purposes. The explanatory system must fit the situation, but fitting is not a mechanical process. Very few of the processes in explanation can be carried out mechanically. The task of fitting a system to an empirical situation spills over into evaluation of systems as explanations—a question reserved, so far as possible, for the following chapter. Here, we will try to establish the minimal criteria for an adequate fit between system and situation. Again, the most useful point of reference is the purpose for which the explanation is to be used.

In the system paradigm of explanation, we are not concerned with the fit between a particular event and a general proposition, but with the degree of isomorphism between a complete system and an empirical situation. Properly loaded, the terms of a system will encompass the classifications in the description and the rules of interaction in the system will parallel the relational propositions in the description. The system is a pattern or overlay that can be placed upon the empirical situation. The empirical situation is always the richer of the two patterns, but the concepts used to load the system serve as a focusing device that blots out some empirical perceptions and allows others to show through. What appears through the conceptual screen provided by the system must coincide with the pattern etched on that screen by the contents of the system. Then, if the pattern included in the system is useful, the logic of the system will be reflected in the empirical situation. If not, the system must be modified or altered, adding or subtracting variables, modifying the concepts used to load the system, or changing the rules of interaction.

In the "fitting" phase of explanation, empirical and logical considerations overlap and intermingle—as elsewhere in the process. Familiarity with the empirical situation in which the event appears, and with similar or identical situations that have appeared before, is necessary if we are to suggest the variables that ought to be included in the system. Manipulation of the logical structure will suggest the consequences of changing the variables or the rules. A good fit requires experience, skill, and perhaps a measure of luck—or insight. Ideally, all of the empirical variables that influence the event to be explained will be included in the system; if a change in the value of any variable will produce a change in the variables that define the event, that variable is relevant. In practice, the question of influence may be uncommonly difficult to decide, particularly in complex situations where there are many variables interacting. Various techniques (multivariate analysis, factor analysis, etc.) may prove useful in the task. One of the real needs in social theory is the development of more courses in statistics that will allow the student to exploit statistical techniques fully in system building and in fitting systems to empirical data. Statistics is not a panacea, of course, but properly taught it can be a significant asset in theoretical work.

If the ideal is a system that encompasses all or most of the significant variables in an empirical situation, the virtues of deliberate oversimplification ought not to be overlooked. All explanations butcher reality in some degree, and the success that economists have had with their butchery is indicative of the value of parsimony in theorizing. The important question is the degree to which oversimplification influences the purposes for which the explanation is used. Purpose makes distortion or incompleteness tolerable, and at the same time provides criteria for defining what will be tolerated. The physician dealing with a badly wounded patient will ignore aspects of the patient's physical condition that have long-range deleterious effects on health if they do not affect survival. The social theorist is well advised to follow the same principle. That requires him to have some purpose, but without one he can only pursue the chimera of a "general" explanation. In theorizing and explanation, expediency *is* virtuous.

Applied mathematics supplies endless examples of the role of purpose in determining tolerable levels of fit between system and empirical situation. The land surveyor uses plane geometry in his work without worrying about the discrepancies between his observations and the idealized system in which the relations used in surveying are calculated. But the flight engineer seeking maximum fuel economy over long distances must find a geometry more closely tied to the curvature of the earth's surface. The cartographer can supply a variety of approximations, but no map, and no geometry, is perfectly isomorphic to the earth's surface in all respects. It depends on the point of view. From a point many miles above the earth, the surface is analogous to an orange peel; the hiker in the mountains would hardly entertain the analogy, or find it entertaining. Yet these various conceptions of the earth's surface are all compatible with "the facts." We choose among them according to our intentions. And the degree of imperfection that can be tolerated in an explanation in physical or social science must be calculated according to the same considerations.

Aberrations and discrepancies

The principal problem in fitting arises when there are aberrations and discrepancies between expected outcomes and the actual results of observation. Since a system is formal and logical and no set of empirical variables is completely isolated from the environment, it is always possible that changes will occur in an empirical situation that cannot be accounted for by an explanatory system, or that changes entailed by an explanatory sytem will not occur in the empirical situation. The application of a system to an empirical situation is always problematic. What is to be done with discrepancies? Ultimately, if discrepancies persist and purposes can no longer be served by the system, it must be modified or replaced. Otherwise it turns into a Procrustean bed into which all manner of data may be forced—with suitable mutilation. But is the system to be modified at the slightest sign of imperfection? Or must it be maintained at all costs until it can be replaced? Neither extreme is tenable; some imperfection is tolerable but too much is not. Purpose allows us to decide.

In this instance, the deductive paradigm is seriously misleading. The widely cited axiom to the effect that a single instance to the contrary is enough to discredit a nomic generalization, taken literally and seriously, is a counsel of despair and not a search for perfection. No one really believes that a discrepancy between the law of gravity and one empirical observation would lead us to abandon the law; the sobriety of the observer, rather than the acceptability of the law, would be questioned. Yet it is statistically possible, if unlikely, that all of the molecules in a given object could, for a small fraction of a second, be moving in the same direction, and the result would certainly defy the law of gravity. More realistically, the results predicted by the law of gravity never appear precisely in observation. If they did, the observer would suspect that he had made some serious errors in measurement. In everyday inquiry, the data *never* fit the explanatory system perfectly; there are always minor errors, exceptions, aberrations. If the fit seems perfect, we need only increase the precision of our measurements and the perfection of fit dissipates rapidly. Some procedure is needed for handling such minor, or even major, variations from expectation.

It is both convenient and useful to deal with discrepancies between system predictions and empirical observations by adding a *ceteris paribus* clause (hereafter abbreviated as *cp*) to the loaded system when it is applied to an empirical situation. Within the system the *cp* is assumed constant and has no effect on system entailments. Exceptions and aberrations in observation, however, can be attributed to the influence of the *cp*, or more precisely, to the influence of the factors (unknown) lodged in the *cp*. Although this may appear a useless contrivance at first glance, it plays a very important role in explanation. For one thing, it allows the theorist to lump together all of the unidentified influences in an empirical situation and deal with them collectively rather than individually— a much easier task. Further, if the influence of the *cp* can be established as a whole, it becomes a useful index to the reliability of the system in explanation. And as disciplines mature and explanatory systems improve, inquiry can concentrate increasingly on the elimination of the *cp* from established systems. Meanwhile, it serves as a useful reminder of the problematic nature of explanation since it can never be wholly eliminated from the system.

The use of the *cp* clause also makes it possible and profitable to use systems that are known to be partial and incomplete. The influence of the *cp* clause on the event to be explained will be larger in systems that are intentionally partial, but that is not always a handicap. For example, if the event to be controlled is of extreme importance, an explanation that provides an imperfect remedy may still be more useful than no explanation at all. And working with an imperfect system provides an opportunity to improve it; comparison of system entailments with the actual results of observation and use, particularly when use is systematic and regulated, can often provide insight into the functioning of the unspecified factors present in the *cp*. A classic illustration of the process is found in the discovery of the planet Pluto. Long before Pluto was observed, it was clear that some major unknown body must lie within the solar system because the behavior of the planets did not correspond exactly to predictions based on the known planets. By extrapolation, a considerable amount of information about the location, etc., of the planet was obtained. In fact, without this information, Pluto might well have escaped notice for some time since it is very difficult to locate with an optical telescope. The *cp* clause does not solve the problem of evaluating discrepancies between system expectations and observations, but it provides us with a very convenient method for dealing with them.

We have not examined the empirical description, the system used in explanation, the concepts used to load the system, and the fit between system and observation. We have an explanation for the event that concerns us if each of these procedures has been properly carried out. However, it is not too difficult to produce a system that *fits* an empirical situation. It is a very different matter to produce an explanation that will *hold for* the event, that can be used to control the event with a known level of confidence. Even if the internal logic of the system is faultless, the description is accurate, and the fit between description and system is excellent, the explanation may still be useless. Changes in weather conditions, for example, may be explained by a system that connects patterns of human behavior to attitudes of a set of deities and patterns of weather to the attitudes of those same deities, according to well-defined rules. When men behave improperly, the gods are angered; when the gods are angered, they send floods, droughts, or other kinds of bad weather to punish man. The system can be linked to empirical indicators so that the human behavior that irks the gods can be identified. The logic of the system can be made impeccable. But the system accounts for weather changes; it does not explain them. We need to look more closely at the reasons why that is so, and to look at the grounds on which systems are established or accepted within a discipline.

CHAPTER FIVE

EVALUATING EXPLANATIONS

THE aim of methodological inquiry is to make explicit, and thereby to help improve, the procedures and instruments through which the human intellect organizes the endless stream of unrelated perceptions that crowds through the gates of consciousness. The concept of explanation proposed here assumes that the organizing apparatus is learned rather than innate, hence that the fundamental cognitive task is to create patterns that can be imposed upon the incoming stream of perceptions in ways that will create understanding of what is being perceived and expectations that will follow—and that will suggest ways in which man can intervene to alter the course of events for his own ends. The procedures and instruments are the same for everyone, rude savage or learned scientist; the difference between personal knowledge and scientific knowledge is substantive and not procedural.

The patterns used in cognitive operations must have certain minimal properties if the criteria of explanation are to be met. The relations implicit in the pattern must be known, finite, and in part calculable; unknowns cannot be used to organize perceptions, and perception of part of a pattern must allow the observer to infer the remainder. The consequences of altering part of the pattern must be determinable, otherwise the structure cannot suggest ways of controlling events. The logical system that performs these functions must be loaded with concepts that have empirical relevance. The expectations generated by such systems are warranted by the logical properties of the calculus; the concepts used to load the system provide the link between system expectations and empirical expectations. Ultimately, the justification for using the system in explanation comes from the results obtained by its use.

An explanation is analogous in many respects to a map. A map records the results of observation, using conventional rules and symbols; it tells us what to expect when certain landmarks are sighted. No map records *everything* in an empirical situation; the map chosen for use should suit the purpose of the user. Maps, like explanations, structure a particular situation from a given point of view. And maps, like explanations, must be altered to include new experience or changes in the situation. Given a purpose, and some knowledge of the way in which the map was prepared, some criticism of the adequacy of the map can be made before the map is used. In the end, the value of the map must be tested by use.

A number of points in an explanation are open to evaluation by simple inspection. The system must be consistent internally and the concepts used to load the system must have empirical relevance. The operation of the rules of interaction must produce results that are compatible with knowledge of the field and in some degree with common sense. No explanation is acceptable in social science, for example, if it incorporates principles that conflict with the laws of motion, or of modern genetic theory. Finally, the rules of correspondence that link the concepts in the explanation to the empirical situation must be stated clearly enough to allow a trained observer to identify an empirical situation as a member of the class of events covered by the explanation. And it must be possible to train observers to make that identification; explanation cannot be contingent upon special insights open to only a few particular (self-appointed?) persons.

ESTABLISHING EXPLANATIONS

The system paradigm of explanation is built upon a loose or weak definition of explanation. Any structure that stipulates the interactions leading to an event and suggests means for controlling it satisfies the minimal criteria. While the definition facilitates discussion of the kinds of explanations that social scientists can produce, it allows the strength and reliability of an explanation to vary greatly. At one extreme, a powerful explanation approximates a deductive explanation; at the other extreme, a weak explanation may be quite unreliable and do no more than suggest minimal control over the event explained. It is not enough, therefore, to establish a system as an explanation, it must also be evaluated—its quality must also be known.

Quality and purpose

I have suggested that evaluation depends for its point of reference on the purposes for which an explanation can be used. No system explanation can be tested "in general," since that would require "the" explanation of an event. When an explanation is very powerful, the reference to purpose can sometimes be dropped since the explanation will then serve almost any purpose to which the event explained might be relevant—the explanation of electricity offered in Chapter Two illustrates the point. But when explanations are weak, they cannot be judged adequate, or established, without taking into consideration the purposes they can serve.

Every explanation suggests ways in which control can in principle be exercised over an empirical situation; that is a definitional requirement. But control is a matter of degree, and no more is implied than the capacity to introduce some change, however minor, into an empirical situation by deliberate action. The amount of control over the situation that is needed to satisfy the purpose for which the explanation is used will vary greatly. It follows that the relation between the amount of control that an explanation permits and the amount that is needed for given purposes will be an important factor when the adequacy of an explanation is being evaluated.

For example, a variety of explanations can be offered for changes in the pattern of income distribution in society over a given time period. If the purpose of the inquirer is to make *some* change occur in the distribution, without regard to type or amount, a simple two-factor explanation linking the incidence of taxation to income distribution may be adequate. If the purpose is sharpened very slightly, say by adding the requirement that the change involve a minimal outlay of resources, the two-factor explanation will not do. All possible ways in which distribution might be changed must now be examined and their respective costs calculated. And if the purpose is to improve the position of the lower third of the income scale without affecting the rate of capital investment, a very powerful explanation will be needed, since the precise amount and kind of change to follow from any particular action will have to be calculated.

In this context, a distinction is needed between explanations for the behavior of aggregates and explanations of individual behavior. In principle, the behavior of aggregates can probably be reduced to individual behavior, but it is often difficult and unnecessary to make the reduction. The distinction is sometimes confused with the difference between explaining an individual event and explaining a class of events. Explanations apply to a class because they apply to each member of the class and not because they apply to individuals. A class of aggregates will have members that are also aggregates. An explanation offered for the behavior of aggregates need make no reference to the individual events that make up the aggregate, though explanations of the two types of events should be compatible. It follows that an explanation for aggregate behavior will provide control in principle over the aggregate and not over the individuals who comprise it, and that interventions in the empirical situation based on an aggregate explanation may have radically different consequences for individuals. A government may introduce a policy designed to improve the position of those in the lower income brackets, for example, that will lead to a serious decline in the incomes of some of the poorly paid even though the policy as a whole is successful. The purposes that can be accomplished using an explanation of aggregate behavior, in other words, are radically different from and even incompatible with the purposes that an explanation of individual behavior can fulfill.

An *established* explanation is a system that has been put to the test; it will explain given events with known reliability and can be used for defined purposes. The explanation may be weak or strong, the range of purposes it will satisfy may be broad or narrow, its reliability may be good or poor. What is important is to be able to specify its quality. When we seek to establish or evaluate an explanation, four points are crucial: first, it must be isomorphic to an empirical situation; second, it must be compatible with other accepted explanations; third, its predictions should be dependable; fourth, the means of intervention it suggests should enable the user to achieve some specifiable purpose.

Isomorphism

An explanation consists of a set of variables and the rules that govern the changes in the values of those variables; each of the variables is loaded with a concept that has empirical relevance. The gist of the explanation is the assertion, warranted by the logic of the system, that one type of change within the system will be accompanied or followed by another. That is, in a very simple case, when the value of one variable increases, an increase in the value of another will follow. The phenomenon to be explained appears as a given change or set of changes within the system. When the explanation is produced, the system is fitted to the empirical situation in which the phenomenon occurs so that variables match descriptive concepts, and rules of interaction parallel relational propositions—rules governing changes in the variables.

The system is never a perfect isomorph for the empirical situation; some events or variables in the empirical world are left out of the explanation. We must begin with the system rather than the empirical situation when an explanation is being tested or evaluated. The variables in the system must be matched within the description;

all remaining empirical variables are included in the *ceteris paribus* clause. Explanations apply to any situation to which they are isomorphic; if the system is matched within the situation, the explanation should apply. The purpose of testing is to determine whether the system produces accurate expectations in other situations where isomorphism can be established. The class of events to which the system applies is defined by the basic terms of the system, and not by external standards.

When a class of events is defined prior to explanation, the explanation may not hold for the entire class. For example, an explanation of changes in income distribution would have to hold for every member of that class of events, and a two-factor explanation linking an increase in wages to a change in the income distribution would account for only part of the class. So long as the class of events covered by an explanation can be identified as a subclass of some larger class defined by other criteria, the explanation for the subclass provides a partial explanation for the large class. If other subclasses can also be explained, it is possible to combine those explanations into a complex system—a system of subsystems—that can deal with the larger class. The system paradigm encourages this procedure since it is unnecessary to have a single set of generalizations that will apply to the entire class of events.

An adequate explanation of changes in income distribution, for example, would require a complex, multivariable system. The number of factors known to relate to income distribution is large: governmental activities such as taxation, transfer payments, or minimum wage laws; economic factors such as wage and price levels; and other factors such as discrimination or restrictive practices, are all relevant to income distribution within society. By breaking down the larger class into subclasses, explanation of the subclasses is simplified in a very useful way. Some changes in income distribution, for example, will be due to transfer payments, and they can be calculated independently; others may be attributed mainly to wage-price ratios. By combining partial explanations it may be possible to provide an explanation for the larger class of events. If the explanations are adequate, all of the requirements of explanation will be met for each subclass, hence the total explanation will also be adequate.

Since system explanations are always partial isomorphs, incomplete explanations cause no particular difficulties. In fact, variables known to be related to a phenomenon are often excluded from an explanatory system (included in the *cp* clause) when their influence is slight, or when their influence cannot be measured. Calculation is impossible if a system contains unknown factors, and nothing is lost through this procedure. Other things equal, it is better to include variables in the system, partly because some may serve as catalysts for other interactions, but also because identification of empirical situations to which the explanation applies is thereby made more accurate.

The value of the *cp* clause is here apparent. It provides, in effect, a single undefined variable which combines all of the influences not specified in the formal system. When the system is tested, we want to know whether the influence of the *cp* clause is too large or variable to permit use of the system for stipulated purposes. And it is sometimes possible to determine the influence of the clause as a whole by examining a number of examples, in which case the influence of the variable is known even though its content cannot be stipulated. As an example, if the explanation used in Chapter Two to deal with electrical phenomenon were modified by eliminating one variable and moving it to the cp clause [taking the form $E = I$ (cp)], a sequence of measurements would soon establish the fact that $(cp) = \dfrac{E}{I}$ and the explanation could then be stabilized, even though the content of cp remained unspecified.

Testing the explanation

When an explanatory system has been fitted to an empirical situation so that the loaded variables are matched within the description, and the changes in the values of the variables predicted by the system are found to occur in the empirical situation, the system provides an explanation for any phenomenon that can be defined within the context of the system. The general procedure to be followed when the system is tested is replication; given another empirical situation in which the variables in the explanatory system are present, does the system's prediction hold for that case as well? Or, to put the question in another form, does the explanation contain a selection of variables sufficiently detached from the surrounding environment to allow their explanation by the system wherever they occur? The only way to answer the question is by testing the system in the empirical world.

This way of constructing explanation accounts for the difficulties we experience with simple two-factor explanations. For the explanation to hold, those two factors would have to be connected to each other strongly enough to override any other connection either might have with the environment. In a Damon and Pythias situation, that might be a reasonable assumption, or in another case, an individual might be so greedy for money that all of the other factors in the situation could be ignored. More commonly, particularly in social science, dyadic relations are rarely so powerful as to exclude all other factors. The relations are dyadic, granted, but the strength of some dyads is greater than others and may vary. That is, any complex set of interactions can be reduced to dyads and the dyads can then be combined, but if the strength of the relation varies within a dyad, the rules of combination also vary. Explanation depends on our capacity to locate stable patterns within these complex relations, on the ability to separate a large enough complex from the environment to permit explanations of what happens within the complex to be couched solely in terms of what the complex includes. A system of four variables, A, B, C, and D, must be separated from the environment, as an entity, to a degree that allows us to discuss the relation between A, B, C, and D solely in terms of A, B, C, and D. The cp clause can be added to deal with minor discrepancies. If the relations among the four elements are stable, rules linking changes in their values can be formulated and explanation is possible.

The purpose of testing, clearly, is to determine the extent to which the variables included in an explanatory set meet these criteria. If the relations predicted by the system hold for the example, that is evidence to the effect that the selection of variables is good. If there is a discrepancy, it may be attributed to minor variations within the system, and therefore included in the influence of the cp clause or it may suggest that the selection of variables should be augmented or altered. To decide the question, we must refer to purpose. If repeated testing shows, for example, that increases in the values of the variables in the empirical situation occur as expected, but that the amount of increase is subject to wide variation, the acceptability of the explanation depends on the compatibility of the variation with the purpose for which the explanation is used. An explanation of the economic factors involved in mineral production, for example, may suggest that a certain governmental policy will lead to an increase in the production of those minerals that the government wishes to encourage, but testing may show that the amount of some minerals will exceed what is needed. Whether the surplus production is regarded as a good reason for rejecting the policy, or as a necessary evil to be tolerated as a price for gaining other ends made possible by the explanation, will depend on the position of the government at the time—on the purposes it wants to achieve and the price it is willing to pay. Testing may also reveal, of course, that an explanation holds extremely well, but that does not automatically qualify the explanation for every purpose. A weak explanation may hold well, but fail to provide the measure of control that is required; in that case, a stronger explanation with lower reliability may be preferred.

Compatibility with other systems.   In addition to tests made against empirical situations, explanations are easily tested against other accepted propositions within the field. Even in a new field, there are always some other explanations that are relevant, and they provide a useful reference point for testing explanations. If the consequences of an explanation conflict with accepted knowledge in any field, one or the other must give way. It cannot be assumed, of course, that what is already established will in every case survive; that would be intellectual conservatism of the worst sort. The account of events to be abandoned is determined by observation and use, not pedigree. The intellectual marketplace is a purely competitive system, in the economist's sense of the terms, and it may very well be the only place on earth where pure competition still holds —or has ever held.

Using history

When explanations are being tested, the social scientist is at a disadvantage compared to his colleague in physical science. Experiments are not readily performed and control over the variables used in explanation is rarely achieved. The social consequences of "natural" testing of explanations may be so serious as to make it unlikely. It is a much more difficult task to establish an explanation in social science than in physical science, and the justification for an explanation will usually be weak. The history of the past, and the record of the future as it unfolds in the present, must provide the bulk of the argument in favor of an explanation. Experimentation, though increasing in importance, is not yet the prime source of verification for social theories.

History is sometimes asserted to be the laboratory of the social sciences and it is assumed as a matter of course that explanations of contemporary events should provide understanding of what has occurred in the past before they can be accepted. That position is too strong. History is useful in social science, but must be used cautiously. There are various ways to account for discrepancies between an explanation and an historical record without discrediting the explanation. The account may be inaccurate or inadequate; historians do not always record the kind of information that social scientists require, nor is their information put in a form in which it is readily accessible and useful. To obtain historical data, we must read history, and that can be a thankless task. Moreover historical accounts are always problematic, as each generation of "revisionists" hastens to inform us. In addition, the event to which the explanation is applied may not be a member of the class of events to which the explanation applies—either the concepts may be improperly defined, or the historical account may be misleading. The same argument holds in the opposite direction: the fact that an explanation holds for an historical instance does not "prove" the adequacy of the explanation, though the capacity to do so is a point in the explanation's favor.

There are limits, in other words, to the importance to be attached to the explanatory capacity of a system when it is applied to the past, and particularly the distant past. For many social scientists, history may prove more useful as a suggestion box, as a source of analogies and structured relationships, rather than as a testing ground for explanations. Without attempting to suggest the best way to squeeze juice from the historian's turnip, the social scientist who is self-consciously aware of his own theoretical needs and interests may find the study of history a most useful device for fertilizing his imagination. The point may be trivial, but we seem at times to be breeding a generation of social scientists with little knowledge of, and even less interest in, history.

Limitations aside, an historical example of the class of events to which an explanation applies can provide a number of points for testing an explanation. Is the selection of variables reflected accurately in the historical account? Does the system explain the event? That is, given the explanation, is the configuration of events in the historical account to be expected? Does the explanation suggest means for altering the event in various ways? Clearly, time-bound or culture-bound explanations cannot be tested in this way. An explanation of the development of the U.S. Senate cannot be tested by reference to the Roman Senate; the explanation would have to be directed at the development of second chambers in legislatures, or some similar class of events, before the data of Roman history would be relevant.

The crux of an explanation is the assertion that certain events will appear in definite patterns, and that changes within those patterns will follow certain rules. History provides an opportunity to test both aspects of explanation. We need to ask whether the patterns appear in the form stipulated by the explanation, and if the changes follow the rules that the explanation proposes. For example, if an explanation asserts that an increase in population will be accompanied by an increase in the size of the bureaucracy, that proposition is readily tested in a variety of situations. And the historical examples may give some indication of the proportionate increase to be expected in each case. The test is always less precise than we would like because the variables in the historical situation cannot be controlled, but it does provide evidence about the acceptability of an explanation that cannot be obtained from any other source. Further, historical cases can sometimes be found that demonstrate the consequences of particular kinds of interventions in given empirical situations and these too, if they parallel the terms of the explanation, provide a test of the viability of the explanation.

The principal danger to be avoided in the use of historical tests of social theory is the "n of instances" fallacy. While it is useful to find some examples of the event that an explanation refers to, the number of examples is far less important than their quality, and the power of the explanation is wholly unrelated to the number of cases that can be located. Increasing examples helps eliminate random variables from the empirical situation, and that is useful for evaluating and clarifying the selection of variables in the explanation. But a weak explanation may hold far more frequently than a strong explanation, indeed is likely to do so. And frequency of occurrence is far less significant than the social consequences of the event when it does occur: floods are less frequent than fires, but often far more disastrous.

Experiment

The ideal way to test any explanation is to reproduce the situation in which the explanation applies, isolated from all other influence. The explanation can then be tested in part and as a whole, and it is usually possible to produce carefully measured observations of the results. In effect, an experiment produces an empirical isomorph for an explanation, eliminating the background variables and producing a "pure" situation. Experiments underscore the importance of the "patterning" procedure involved in explanation. That is, an explanation is an explication of the interactions that occur among a set of organized variables, extracted from the surroundings. In the natural environment, the separation of pattern and environment is incomplete and problematic; in an experimental situation, it is much more precisely achieved. For these reasons, experimental evidence provides the most precise test possible of the validity of an explanation. And since it offers a base for comparing the operation of a system in isolation and the operation of a system in its natural environment, it can give us information about the interactions between the system as a whole and the environment that cannot be obtained in any other way.

The virtues of laboratory experiments are well known. The dangers should also be noted briefly. Excessive reliance upon laboratory results, best exemplified by some branches of psychology in the 1930's, may be grossly misleading, particularly when there is a serious discrepancy between natural conditions and laboratory conditions. The aim of explanation is to help man to cope with his environment and the results of laboratory experiment are not, strictly speaking, applicable to the environment without modification. Success in the laboratory may convince us that a given system provides a very precise explanation for a given class of events, yet that explanation may be useless for either understanding or controlling events when it is applied outside the laboratory. If interfering conditions are so frequent that a laboratory-tested explanation will not function properly, it is wise to change the terms of the explanation to take such interfering conditions into account rather than stick to an explanation that cannot meet the criteria of explanation in the empirical world outside the laboratory.

Social scientists have made considerable progress in the development of experimental techniques in recent years—some more than others, of course. But the "natural" experiment remains the prime source of information in most cases. By acting on an explanation in the present, we obtain information about the quality of the explanation by observing the consequences of the actions. Are the expectations generated by the explanation fulfilled? Do interventions suggested by the explanation produce the anticipated results? The results are rarely perfect. Even so widely "tested" a set of explanations as Keynesian economics remains untested in certain essentials—it has never been demonstrated, for example, that governments are really able to inhibit the decline of national income solely by monetary and fiscal policies.

The possibility of such "natural" experiments has not been exploited fully, particularly in political science and sociology, partly, no doubt, out of fear of the consequences of "social engineering," but also because social scientists have tended to define their functions in other terms. Few political scientists, for example, think of government as a testing ground for their theories. Though the spread of governmental activity has often forced social science into active experimentation, many social scientists regard such activity with distaste. Yet the opportunities for developing theories in education, welfare, urbanization, and numerous other problem areas in modern society are virtually endless—and there are numerous sources of funds that might be used for that purpose.

One final source of information about the viability of an explanation is the development of corollary and related explanations within the field. New theories often provide an argument in favor of other theories in quite different fields. The strength of learning theory may be increased by developments in neurophysiology or sociology as well as in psychology. Our confidence in a particular explanation for some aspect of group behavior may be strengthened by observations or explanations based on the behavior of groups of primates or other animals. There is no rule, of course, for evaluating such information, yet it sometimes plays an important part in the discussion that establishes explanations.

The aim of testing, or any other activity designed to establish an explanation, is to increase the level of confidence we feel in the explanation. No explanation, whether in physical or social science, can be established beyond all argument. The question is: How convincing is the evidence? Under what conditions are we willing to use it? The drowning man will clutch at straws, and in the absence of *any* explanation, a weak structure may seem better than none; that is not always so, however, and an uncertain cure may be worse than the disease. Few explanations in social science are presently so well established that they can be used as models for the future, and the explanations in physical science are not a good model because their quality is rarely matched in social science. In part, at least, the weakness of explanations in social science can be attributed to their short history; the explanations that 18th-century physical scientists accepted are not always impressive by contemporary standards either. Evaluation of explanations, as explanations, has barely started in social science. Systematic explanation is itself a relatively recent innovation, particularly in political science and even sociology. New standards of measurement are badly needed, and will do much to improve the quality of explanation when they are produced. New concepts are almost bound to appear that will improve on those now available. Meanwhile, we can do no more than use the tools we have and try to improve them or devise new ones. The principal goal at this juncture ought probably to be the development of agreement on the goals of inquiry, on the proper relation between the normative and explanatory aspects of inquiry, and on the ways in which those goals might be fulfilled. The important thing is to be aware of the need for explanations, to understand what makes for good explanations, and to seek improvements in the explanatory structure with such resources as can be mobilized.

EVALUATING EXPLANATIONS

Beyond the question of whether an explanation holds for a given class of phenomena, various other qualities of explanation need to be taken into consideration. Examination of these qualities will be called *evaluation* to distinguish it from the procedures used to establish the explanation. The purpose of evaluation is to assess the usefulness of an explanation. Four points are particularly important: first, the *scope* of the explanation, the range of events to which it can be applied; second, explanations differ in *precision*, in the accuracy of the expectations they generate and of the control procedures they imply; third, explanations differ in *power*, in the amount of control over an empirical situation that they permit; finally, explanations differ in *reliability*, in the amount of confidence we place on their use. The purposes that an explanation can serve will usually be defined by these four properties. Ideally, an explanation will have a wide scope, precision, power, and reliability, but certain purposes can usually be served if one or more of these factors is weak.

Scope

The scope of an explanation, the range of events that it can explain, depends primarily on the concepts used to load the system. Other things being equal, explanations should be as wide as possible, should have a "high" level of generality. In physical science, enormous scope has often been combined with great precision, but in the social sciences it has not usually been possible to produce this combination. Widening the scope of an explanation has usually meant loosening the defining terms of the concepts used to load the system—running the risk of ambiguity. Systems loaded with psychiatric concepts, for example, are usually applicable to a wide range of human actions, but it is often very difficult to obtain unambiguous expectations from their use. A system loaded with biographical data, on the other hand, is quite accurate but not very helpful.

Social science already possesses a number of concepts that have a very wide scope, and seem amenable to theoretical use—"role," "choice," "value," and so on, are quite promising theoretically. But other terms are uncommonly difficult to operationalize: "stability," "power," "authority," or "legitimacy" are good examples. The physical sciences have managed to achieve conceptual precision and wide scope mainly by limiting their concepts to time and/or dimensionality, and that is not a limitation that social science can accept, at the moment at least. The problem cannot be solved here, but it seems clear that a good deal of attention must be devoted to conceptionalization if social science is to produce adequate explanations with a wide scope without sacrificing accuracy and precision.

One possibility that can be suggested, though not explored, is greater concentration on the kinds of behavior that occur in structured social situations—what is implied in "structural-functional" analysis, with some modifications. It is strikingly easy to explain the behavior of individual players during the course of a baseball game by referring to the rules of the game. Much significant human behavior occurs in analogous situations, though the degree of structuring may be substantially less. An exploration of the social analogs to game situations might produce some very useful results—if only to demonstrate the limits on the use of that kind of explanation. An examination of the kinds of concepts that are used to explain heavily structured behavior might, moreover, throw a great deal of light on the conceptualization problem in social science. And if the baseball audience is taken into consideration, the effect of differential structuring can then be examined, together with the conditions that maintain such differentials—and the conditions under which they break down, and a melee ensues.

Precision

The precision of an explanation refers to the exactness with which the concepts used in explanation are related to empirical indicators, and the precision with which the rules of interaction of the variables in the system are stated. The ideal, clearly, is precisely measured expectations specified in terms of standard units of measurements on an interval or ratio scale, if only because such measurements can be manipulated mathematically. The critical point here is the accuracy of the description, the quality of measurements in which the description is stated.

Unfortunately, as everyone who has tried it knows, measurements in social science are difficult to make, and many social scientists feel that social phenomena are in fact beyond precise measurement. Admittedly, the obstacles to exact measurement are greater in social than in physical science but there seems no reason in principle why the quality cannot be improved. Time and magnitude can be measured very precisely, using indicators borrowed from physical science, but social scientists have developed very few indicators that can be defined in terms of magnitude and time. Interest in social measurement has increased greatly since the 1950's, and some of the recent works in the field are worth close attention, not because they solve all of our problems of measurement, but because they suggest how much can be done with the tools already available.[1]

Power

How much control over the environment does an explanation provide? The range is great: a weak explanation may do no more than suggest a way of altering events without stipulating the nature of the outcome, while an explanation that includes the necessary and sufficient conditions for an event, stipulated in precisely measured terms, may provide control over the event that is nearly perfect. In the simplest case (no ϕ unless A) the event may be prevented by eliminating one or more necessary conditions, and *perhaps* facilitated by ensuring its presence. The explanation used in Chapter Two, on the other hand, may provide predictions valid to several decimal places. Power, in other words, depends on the precision of the description, the precision of the explanation, and the *completeness* of the explanation. An explanation that includes *all* variables known to relate to a given

---

[1]One of the best is Aaron C. Cicourel, *Method and Measurement in Sociology* (Free Press, 1964); but see also Eugene J. Webb, Donald T. Campbell, Richard D. Schwartz and Lee Sechrist, *Unobtrusive Measures: Nonreactive Research in the Social Sciences* (Rand, McNally, 1966), or Raymond A. Bauer (ed.), *Social Indicators* (M.I.T. Press, 1966), especially Albert D. Biderman's essay "Social Indicators and Goals." For an older essay, see C. Coombs, "Theory and Methods of Social Measurement," in L. Festinger and D. Katz, *Research Methods in the Behavioral Sciences* (Holt, Rinehart & Winston, 1953).

event, and the rules that link them together, is much more powerful, other things being equal, than an explanation that places some of its known variables in the *cp* clause because it cannot stipulate the manner in which they interact in the system.

Reliability

The application of an explanatory system to an empirical situation is always problematic; that is the reason for including a *cp* clause in loaded systems when they are applied. It is not merely a case of having an inadequate explanation, an explanation which fails to include known variables; even if the explanation is as exact as we can make it, the problem of uncertainty is still present. Imagine an immense stage on which many different plays are being performed. The observer is analogous to a spectator in the theater armed with a pair of spectacles that enable him to see one of the plays but not the others. However perfectly the spectacles may be ground, it is always possible that what is going on in one play will influence the others. Reliability of explanations has to do with the frequency with which such disturbances or discrepancies occur. They are revealed by observation and use only. Over time, the results obtained from the use of an explanation give us information about its reliability to the extent that they permit us to specify the frequency with which factors not included in the explanation interfere with the empirical situation that the explanation refers to.

Reliability cannot be an absolute figure; some reference must be made to the purpose for which an explanation is used. A system may be reliable for some purposes but useless for others. An explanation of some aspect of economic activity, for example, may aid in the suppression of economic depressions but provide no assistance whatever when the general level of economic activity is to be expanded.

Usually, reliability can be increased by decreasing the precision of the explanation. A system that is unreliable when stated in terms of interval measurements may be quite reliable when ordinal measures are used. Here, as elsewhere in explanation, we must choose among qualities according to our needs. As the precision of an explanation increases, reliability will eventually begin to decrease. An optimum point must be selected, a level of precision that will provide the accuracy that is needed with sufficient reliability. The choice will be made, obviously enough, within the limits defined by purpose.

Postscript

The procedures by which social scientists can establish and evaluate their explanations are far from perfect, even under ideal conditions. The choice seems to lie between accepting a conception of explanation that is so strict that social science cannot satisfy it, as in the deductive paradigm of explanation, and accepting a conception that is broader but destroys the homogeneity of explanations and forces us into the difficult process of evaluation. This essay argues for the latter, primarily because it appears that the introduction of purpose into the criteria of explanation will in practice make for a workable solution to the problem. That does not mean that there will not be quarrels about the adequacy of an explanation, or disputes about their other qualities. Some may prove insoluble. But the weaker definition of explanation makes a systematic beginning feasible, provides a base for codifying what is already known in the social sciences in a form that is useful; and that seems the principal need at the present time. We must somehow stabilize the point of departure for our students, and suggest the nature of the route that systematic inquiry must travel. There can be no guarantee of success, of course, but neither is there any necessary reason for assuming failure in advance.

CHAPTER SIX

REPRISE

THE system paradigm of explanation is not meant as a panacea; its use carries no guarantees of success. It has two virtues: practicality and conceptual simplicity. It makes possible the systematic pursuit of explanations and the systematic application of explanations in social science without recourse to the unfulfillable need for "general laws." A single paradigm suffices for explanations in all fields, and it seems to accord well with the actual working practices of social and physical scientists. It avoids a number of logical and conceptual difficulties that arise within the deductive paradigm. The one major problem involved in its use is the need to introduce qualitative distinctions among explanations, but if that may prove difficult it is by no means impossible to do.

The logical and conceptual puzzles created by the fusion of the logical and empirical aspects of explanation are avoided, thereby simplifying the explanatory process considerably. The search for "empirical generalizations" is abandoned. The cost to the social scientist is small since his generalizations were in any case inadequate for deductive explanation and they are readily incorporated into systems as logical propositions. Instead of searching for a carefully defined niche for each element in an observation, we search for patterns that seem to fit empirical situations in part—a reasonable goal for social science. The troublesome problem of induction is bypassed quite effectively. And perhaps most important of all, due weight is given to both logical skill and empirical knowledge in the explanatory process.

The structure of explanations is much simplified by the use of the system paradigm. This distinction between deductive and probabilistic explanations, so important in the deductive paradigm, disappears. All systems are constructed in the same way, and the terms in which events are described are irrelevant to the form of explanation. Within a system, operations are always formal and deductive. When systems are applied to empirical situations, the criteria employed are pragmatic rather than logical. The reliability of a given system for a given purpose may be expressed as a fraction but that involves no conceptual difficulties.

Similarly, the complex classification of explanations according to their substantive content, which appears in most works on the methodology of the social sciences— including my own—is no longer needed. Whether the terms in a system are loaded with variables that are "causal," "genetic," "teleological," or "functional" does not matter so long as rules of correspondence can be supplied and the concepts identified empirically. Of course, it may in practice prove more difficult to meet system requirements with some concepts than with others, but that should serve only to reduce ambiguity in conceptualization and eliminate worthless "explanations" in which events are accounted for rather than explained.

Some of the implications of the system paradigm are extremely interesting. It suggests, for one thing, that the tendency to formalization and "model building" in the successful disciplines, the use of applied mathematics, in fact accounts for their success. Explanation is a form of applied mathematics, a form of calculation. That being the case, a careful inquiry into the kinds of calculations that people actually employ in their interactions with others is commended as sound strategy. Both the explainer and the person whose behavior is explained calculate in the same way, though their tools are substantively different. That being the case, logic suggests that a great deal of human behavior might be explicable if the mode of calculation used by individuals, the basic scoring system, could be made explicit. The system paradigm, in other words, tends to focus attention on the *structured* aspects of human behavior or social interaction in general.

Further, the paradigm suggests the usefulness of creating systems that are known oversimplifications—partial or incomplete systems—and then refining them through observation, experiment, and application. The *ceteris paribus* clause in the applied system serves as a flexible and useful device for employing such systems. Even a two-variable system, a single-factor explanation, denounced since the days of Max Weber as prima facie unsound, may in fact be made into a useful tool by adding the *cp* clause. If the influence of the single factor outweighs the influence of the combined elements in the *cp* clause, the resulting oversimplification may serve useful purposes. And in combination, such simplifications can add up to a powerful explanation for a complex and heterogeneous class of events.

Finally, the system paradigm offers the possibility that

the three basic goals of inquiry—description, explanation, and evaluation, can be brought together into a single conceptual framework. Within the paradigm, the interaction of description and explanation is clear; but the paradigm also suggests the role of social evaluation as a guide for the direction of inquiry into useful channels. Much more work is needed to determine the way in which evaluations might be made so that agreement on the outcome proves possible. Even if a problem proved insoluble, a useful clarification of interrelations should be achieved. If the system paradigm does no more than help redefine the problems of inquiry, and perhaps stimulate discussion of the way in which the fundamental methodological problems of social science ought to be attacked, it will have served its purpose well.

INDEX

127

This book has been set in 11 point Caledonia, leaded 2 points, and 10 point Caledonia, leaded 1 point. Chapter numbers are 10 point News Gothic Bold Condensed and chapter titles are 18 point News Gothic Condensed. The size of the type page is 23 by 37½ picas.